HUMAN ANATOMY AND PHYSIOLOGY

An Experimental Handbook

For
B. Pharm Students

Vishnu N. Thakare

Assistant Professor
Department of Pharmacology
Sinhgad Institute of Pharmaceutical Sciences
Kusgaon (Bk), Lonavala-Pune 410401,
India

HUMAN ANATOMY AND PHYSIOLOGY

ISBN 978-93-83750-85-6

Second Edition : November 2015

© : Author

The text of this publication, or any part thereof, should not be reproduced or transmitted in any form or stored in any computer storage system or device for distribution including photocopy, recording, taping or information retrieval system or reproduced on any disc, tape, perforated media or other information storage device etc., without the written permission of Author with whom the rights are reserved. Breach of this condition is liable for legal action.

Every effort has been made to avoid errors or omissions in this publication. In spite of this, errors may have crept in. Any mistake, error or discrepancy so noted and shall be brought to our notice shall be taken care of in the next edition. It is notified that neither the publisher nor the author or seller shall be responsible for any damage or loss of action to any one, of any kind, in any manner, therefrom.

Published By :
NIRALI PRAKASHAN
Abhyudaya Pragati, 1312, Shivaji Nagar,
Off J.M. Road, PUNE – 411005
Tel - (020) 25512336/37/39, Fax - (020) 25511379
Email : niralipune@pragationline.com

Printed By :
Repro Knowledgecast Limited,
Thane

☞ DISTRIBUTION CENTRES

PUNE
Nirali Prakashan : 119, Budhwar Peth, Jogeshwari Mandir Lane, Pune 411002, Maharashtra
Tel : (020) 2445 2044, 66022708, Fax : (020) 2445 1538
Email : bookorder@pragationline.com, niralilocal@pragationline.com

Nirali Prakashan : S. No. 28/27, Dhyari, Near Pari Company, Pune 411041
Tel : (020) 24690204 Fax : (020) 24690316
Email : dhyari@pragationline.com, bookorder@pragationline.com

MUMBAI
Nirali Prakashan : 385, S.V.P. Road, Rasdhara Co-op. Hsg. Society Ltd.,
Girgaum, Mumbai 400004, Maharashtra
Tel : (022) 2385 6339 / 2386 9976, Fax : (022) 2386 9976
Email : niralimumbai@pragationline.com

☞ DISTRIBUTION BRANCHES

JALGAON
Nirali Prakashan : 34, V. V. Golani Market, Navi Peth, Jalgaon 425001,
Maharashtra, Tel : (0257) 222 0395, Mob : 94234 91860

KOLHAPUR
Nirali Prakashan : New Mahadvar Road, Kedar Plaza, 1st Floor Opp. IDBI Bank
Kolhapur 416 012, Maharashtra. Mob : 9850046155

NAGPUR
Pratibha Book Distributors : Above Maratha Mandir, Shop No. 3, First Floor,
Rani Jhanshi Square, Sitabuldi, Nagpur 440012, Maharashtra
Tel : (0712) 254 7129

DELHI
Nirali Prakashan : 4593/21, Basement, Aggarwal Lane 15, Ansari Road, Daryaganj
Near Times of India Building, New Delhi 110002
Mob : 08505972553

Bengaluru
Pragati Book House : House No. 1, Sanjeevappa Lane, Avenue Road Cross,
Opp. Rice Church, Bengaluru – 560002.
Tel : (080) 64513344, 64513355,Mob : 9880582331, 9845021552
Email:bharatsavla@yahoo.com

CHENNAI
Pragati Books : 9/1, Montieth Road, Behind Taas Mahal, Egmore,
Chennai 600008 Tamil Nadu, Tel : (044) 6518 3535,
Mob : 94440 01782 / 98450 21552 / 98805 82331,
Email : bharatsavla@yahoo.com

niralipune@pragationline.com | www.pragationline.com

Also find us on www.facebook.com/niralibooks

Preface

It is with great pleasure that I introduce the book **"Human Anatomy and Physiology – An Experimental Handbook"**. The book allows for the lucid understanding of human anatomy and physiology, which is extremely necessary for the clear understanding of the pathophysiology of various disorders/diseases and effects or actions of drugs. This book is a sincere attempt to explain the basics of human anatomy and physiology in a simple and interesting manner and as per the syllabus prescribed for the first year B. Pharm students by the University of Pune. This book imparts insight into each experiment along with its clinical and pathological significance. Questions that could be asked for viva-voce are also included at the end of each experiment.

All efforts have been made to keep the text error-free and to present the subject in a student friendly and easy to understand manner. However, any suggestions and constructive comments would be highly appreciated and incorporated in the next edition.

Vishnu N. Thakare

Acknowledgements

I feel indebted to Hon. Prof. M. N. Navale (Founder President), Dr. (Mrs.) Sunanda M. Navale (Secretary) Sinhgad Technical Education Society, Pune for their continuous encouragement and support.

I am sincerely grateful to Dr. S. R. Naik (Head of Department, Pharmacology), Dr. S. B. Bhise, Principal, Sinhgad Institute of Pharmaceutical Sciences, Lonavala, for their support, help and guidance.

I express my sincere gratitude to Dr. K. S. Jain, Sinhgad Institute of Pharmaceutical Sciences, Lonavala; Dr. (Mrs.) Bhoomika M. Patel, Nirma Institute of Pharmacy, Ahmedabad; Dr. Niraj Vyawahare, D. Y. Patil College of Pharmacy Pune; Dr. M. M. Ghaisa, Indira College of Pharmacy Pune; Dr. Sohan Chitlange, Dr. D.Y. Patil Institute of Pharm. Sciences, Pune; Dr. R. V. Patil and Dr. N. S. Bhajipale, College of Pharmacy Akola and Mrs. Anupama Suralkar for their continuous help, valuable guidance and advice.

I also express my gratitude to my colleagues Dr. Valmik Dhakane, Mr. R. R. Patil, Mr. R. R. Wadekar, Mr. M. K. Aswar, Mr. Y. P. Kulkarni, Ms. D. K. Ingawale, and Mr. P. G. Pandhare, for their help and support during writing of this book.

My special thanks to my wife Vaishali and my students, Ms. Malvika and Ms. Sanyogita Navale for their kind help.

I express my thanks to Mr. S. B. Gokhale and staff of Nirali Prakashan.

I am also thankful to Mr. Jignish Furia of Nirali Prakashan for publishing this book.

Vishnu N. Thakare

Contents

1. STUDY OF MICROSCOPE — 1-4

EXPERIMENTS ON BLOOD

2. DETERMINATION OF HAEMOGLOBIN CONTENT AND OXYGEN CARRYING CAPACITY OF BLOOD SAMPLE — 5-10
3. DETERMINATION OF THE NUMBER OF RBCs AND COLOUR INDEX OF BLOOD — 11-16
4. STUDY OF OSMOTIC FRAGILITY OF RBCs — 17-20
5. DETERMINATION OF THE NUMBER OF WBCs IN BLOOD SAMPLE — 21-24
6. DETERMINATION OF DIFFERENTIAL LEUKOCYTE COUNT OF BLOOD — 25-28
7. DETERMINATION OF PLATELET COUNT OF BLOOD — 29-32
8. DETERMINATION OF RETICULOCYTE COUNT OF BLOOD — 33-36
9. DETERMINATION OF ARNETH COUNT OF BLOOD — 37-40
10. DETERMINATION OF ERYTHROCYTE SEDIMENTATION RATE — 41-42
11. DETERMINATION OF BLOOD GROUP — 43-46
12. DETERMINATION OF HEMATOCRIT CONTENT OF BLOOD — 47-48
13. DETERMINATION OF BLEEDING TIME AND CLOTTING TIME OF BLOOD — 49-50
14. DETERMINATION OF BLOOD PRESSURE — 51-54
15. RECORDING OF PULSE RATE — 55-56
16. RECORDING OF ELECTROCARDIOGRAM — 57-58
17. MEASUREMENT OF BODY TEMPERATURE — 59-60
18. DETERMINATION AND RECORDING OF RESPIRATORY VOLUME — 61-64
19. DETERMINATION OF BREATH HOLDING TIME AND HYPERVENTILATION TIME — 65-68
20. DETERMINATION OF VISUAL ACUITY FOR NEAR AND DISTANCE VISION — 69-72
21. DETERMINATION OF DOMINANCE OF EYE — 73-73
22. DETERMINATION OF SPECIAL SENSES — 74-76

EXPERIMENTS ON CELL, TISSUES AND BODY SYSTEMS

23. STUDY OF HUMAN CELLS, TISSUES AND HISTOLOGY OF ORGANS — 77-86
24. STUDY OF THE CARDIOVASCULAR SYSTEM — 87-94
25. STUDY OF THE DIGESTIVE SYSTEM — 95-102

26.	STUDY OF THE RESPIRATORY SYSTEM	103-106
27.	STUDY OF THE URINARY SYSTEM	107-110
28.	STUDY OF THE HUMAN SKULL	111-114
29.	STUDY OF THE PECTORAL GIRDLE AND BONES OF THE UPPER LIMB	115-120
30.	STUDY OF BONES OF THE VERTEBRAL COLUMN	121-124
31.	STUDY OF THE PELVIC GIRDLE AND THE LOWER LIMB	125-128
32.	STUDY OF VARIOUS JOINTS	129-134
33.	STUDY OF THE CENTRAL NERVOUS SYSTEM	135-140
34.	STUDY OF THE LYMPHATIC SYSTEM	141-143

EXPERIMENTS ON REPRODUCTIVE SYSTEM

35.	STUDY OF THE MALE REPRODUCTIVE SYSTEM	144-146
36.	STUDY OF THE FEMALE REPRODUCTIVE SYSTEM	147-150
37.	STUDY OF THE HUMAN EYE	151-153
38.	STUDY OF THE HUMAN EAR	154-156
39.	STUDY OF THE HUMAN SKIN	157-159
40.	PREGNANCY DIAGNOSTIC TEST	160-161
41.	STUDY OF FAMILY PLANNING METHODS AND DEVICES	162-165

BIOCHEMICAL ANALYSIS OF URINE

| 42. | BIOCHEMICAL ANALYSIS OF URINE | 166-169 |

EXPERIMENTS ON NERVE MUSCLE PREPARATION (OF FROGS)

43.	STUDY OF THE SIMPLE MUSCLE TWITCH	170-172
44.	EFFECT OF TEMPERATURE ON SIMPLE MUSCLE TWITCH	173-174
45.	STUDY OF FATIGUE ON GASTROCNEMIUS SCIATIC NERVE MUSCLE (OF FROG)	175-176
	• APPENDIX	177-178
	• GLOSSARY	179-185
	• BIBLIOGRAPHY	186-186

EXPERIMENT NO. 1

STUDY OF MICROSCOPE

- **Aim**

  To study the microscope

- **Microscope**

  Microscope is an optical instrument which uses visible light and a system of lenses to view magnified images of very small objects. This microscope also called light microscope.

- **Types**

  (a) Simple microscope – has one set of lens and low magnification.

  (b) Compound microscope – has two sets of lenses and objectives with higher magnifications.

  (c) Electron microscope – This microscope differs from optical microscope; in that the electrons interact with the sample to generate image instead of light acting as an illuminating source.

  For general experiments of physiology, the compound microscope is used for the study of morphological characteristics of blood cells. Compound microscope works on the principle of formation of an enlarged image of sample / object in the plane of focus.

- **Physical terms**

  (a) **Compound microscope :** It is an arrangement of objective and eyepiece used to magnify an object to the point where it can be seen with the human eye.

  (b) **Resolution :** The resolution of an optical microscope is defined as the shortest distance between two points on a specimen that can still be distinguished by the observer as separate entities. Consequently it describes how small objects can lie close to each other and can still be recognisable. Resolution with human eye is around 0.25 mm, with light microscope it is around 0.25 µm and with the electron microscope it is 0.5 nm.

  (c) **Working distance :** It is the distance between the objective lens and the specimen. The magnifications increase with decrease in working distance. The ideal working distance is 0.15-1.5 mm for the oil immersion objective, 0.5-4 mm for high power objective and 5-15 mm for low power objective.

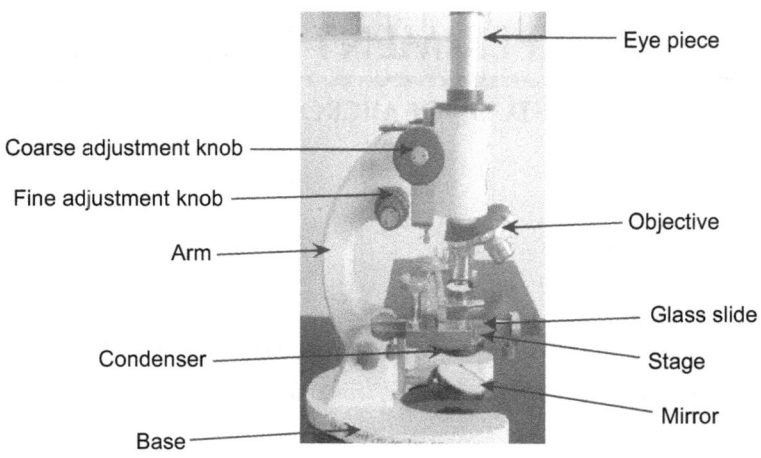

Figure 1.1 : A Compound Microscope

➤ **Parts of a Compound Microscope**

(1) The support system

(2) The illuminating system

(3) The magnification system

(4) The adjustment system.

1. **The Support system:** The support system consists of various parts which are described below.

    (a) Base of microscope: It is horse shoe shaped and is the base on which the microscope rests.

    (b) Pillars: Projecting upward from the base, it is joined to the handle of microscope

    (c) Handle (arm) : Handle is curved shaped or 'c' shaped and supports the magnifying and the adjusting system.

    (d) Body tube : It is the tube which houses the lenses and through which light passes to form an image.

    (e) Stage : It is a horizontal platform on which the specimen under observation is placed. Fixed and mechanical stage microscopes are generally used. The specimen is mounted on a slide which is held in place by clips that are present on the stage. The screws enable the movement of the slide sideways or vertically.

Nosepiece : It is the part of the microscope that holds the objective lenses. It is also called as a revolving nosepiece or turret. Nosepiece is attached to the lower end of the body tube and consists of objective lenses of different magnifications attached to it. The objective of required magnitude can be focused over the specimen by moving the nose piece.

2. The illuminating system : A good illuminating system is the one which provides uniform and bright illumination of the entire field viewed under the microscope.

There are six types of illuminating systems based on which the microscope functions.

(a) Bright field microscope –the source of illumination used is white light, either external sunlight or internal tungsten filament lamp.

(b) Dark field microscope – dark field condenser is used to block scattered light

(c) Fluorescent microscope – UV lamp is used as light source.

(d) The illuminating system of a compound microscope is composed of a light source, a condenser, and a diaphragm.

Mirror is fixed at the base and is used to reflect light from an external light source up through the bottom of the stage. As the rays of light are reflected by mirror through the condenser on the object, the object on the stage appears clear.

Condenser – the rays of light reflected by the mirror pass through the condenser located in between the mirror and stage of the microscope, then fall onto the object under examination and thus help in resolving the image. The position of the condenser needs to be adjusted with each object used in order to alter the light and to improve the resolving power of the microscope.

3. Magnification system: As the name indicates, it directly implies magnifying the image of the object under observation and comprises of the eyepiece and objectives.

(a) Eye piece: The eyepiece is a lens that fits into the top of the body. It magnifies the image formed by the objectives; generally 5x and 10x eyepieces are used. Monocular microscope uses one eyepiece; where as binocular microscope has provision for fitting 2 eyepieces. The magnification formed by the eyepiece multiplied by objective magnification gives the total magnification of the object being viewed.

Objectives : Generally these objectives are screwed into the resolving nosepiece in a compound microscope. The nosepiece is a pivot that ensures quick changes of objectives.

(1) 10X - low power objective- magnifies the image ten times.

(2) 40 or 45X - high power objective- magnifies images 40 or 45 times. It is used for a broad view of blood films or histological sections prior to their examination under oil-immersion objectives.

(3) **Oil-immersion objective (100X)** - This requires immersion oil viz, cedar wood oil. Oil is employed to increase the numerical aperture (is a ratio of the diameter of lens to its focal length) and the resolving power of the objectives. Light passes through glass at same speed as it travels through the immersion oil. Hence, the ray of light that passes through oil undergoes minimum diffraction when it passes through glass. As a result the resulting image is much clearer and sharper.

4. **Adjusting system:** Two adjustment systems are used

(a) Coarse adjustment-Two coarse adjustment screws are employed for coarse adjustment. These screws are mounted at the top of the handle by a double side micrometer mechanism, one on each side.

(b) Fine adjustment-Two fine adjustment screws are mounted on the handle below the coarse adjustment screws by double side micrometer mechanism, one on each side.

EXERCISE

(a) Give the principle of microscope.

(b) Enlist the various parts of a compound microscope.

(c) What is resolution? Give its significance.

(d) State the importance of condenser and iris diaphragm

(e) Give the role of illuminating system in a microscope.

(f) Give the significance of oil used in oil immersion objectives.

EXPERIMENT NO. 2

DETERMINATION OF HAEMOGLOBIN CONTENT AND OXYGEN CARRYING CAPACITY OF BLOOD SAMPLE

➤ Aim

To determine the haemoglobin (Hb) content and oxygen carrying capacity of one's own blood sample.

➤ Apparatus

Sahli's Hellige haemoglobinometer (Figure 2.1), stirrer, micropipette (200 cubic millimeter), disposable needle (24 gauge), Pipette-having single mark 0.02 ml (20 cu nm) without any bulb, 0.1N HCL, 70% alcohol or spirit, cotton, distilled water.

Sahli's haemoglobinometer consists of comparator, tube, pipette and stirrer.

Comparator-the haemoglobinometer at the center point is provided with opening which holds the haemoglobin tube. Two non fading standard brown tubes are provided on both sides of the central haemoglobin glass tube for colour matching.

Tube- Gram% markers on one side up to 30 and % mark (20-140) on another side for easy reading.

➤ Principle

Reaction of blood with hydrochloric acid (HCl) causes the formation of hematin acid by hydrolysis of haemoglobin. Acid hematin is reddish brown in colour. This is then diluted with distilled water until its colour matches exactly with that of the permanent standard of the comparator block. Matching of sample with standard tubes gives exact concentration of haemoglobin of sampled blood.

➤ Theory

Haemoglobin (Hb) is a protein comprising of heme and globin present in RBCs, which carries oxygen and carbon dioxide. Heme portion is involved in transportation of oxygen from lungs to the tissue. Oxyhaemoglobin is the combination of oxygen (4) with one molecule of haemoglobin.

1 gram of Hb carries 1.34ml of oxygen. Haemoglobin also acts as a buffer by maintaining blood pH.

➢ Normal Range

Adult male :   14-18 gm% of blood

Adult female : 12-16 gm% of blood

In newborn :   16-22 gm%

Infants :   12-40 gm%

➢ Procedure

1. Take Sahli's haemoglobinometer and pipette and make sure that it is dry.
2. Fill the haemoglobinometer up to its lowest mark 10% (2 gram %) by adding 0.1N HCL with the help of a dropper.
3. Sterilise the finger tip with spirit or 70% alcohol and prick the finger tip with a sterile needle to allow free flow of blood.
4. Allow a large drop of blood to form on the finger tip, dip the tip of pipette on to the blood drop and suck up to 0.02 ml mark taking care to avoid the formation of an air bubble.
5. Transfer immediately 0.02 ml blood into the haemoglobinometer (containing 0.1N HCL) by blowing pipette.
6. Leave the solution in the tube haemoglobinometer for about 10min.
7. After 10 min, dilute the solution with distilled water, drop by drop and mix it with a stirrer. Keep adding water until colour of solution in the tube matches with standard of the comparator (while matching the two colours, take care to hold the stirrer above the level of the solution).
8. Note the reading when the colour of solution matches to the standard and express the haemoglobin concentration as gram%.

➢ Precaution

Following precautions to be taken while performing this experiment.

1. Blood should be immediately transferred from pipette into haemoglobinometer tube to prevent clotting of blood in the tube.

2. 10 min should be given after addition of blood into haemoglobinometer tube, for complete conversion of haemoglobin to acid hematin.

Result : The haemoglobin content of the blood sample was found to be ...... gm%.

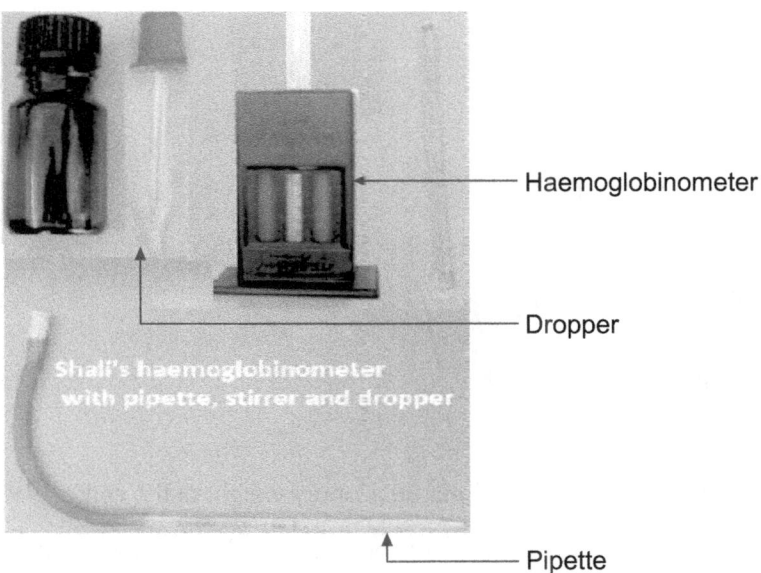

Figure 2.1 : SAHLI'S Haemoglobinometer

➤ Calculation

Observed reading of haemoglobin ------ gm%.

Percentage of haemoglobin

$$14.5 \text{ gms Hb} = 100\%.$$

Observed Hb value = ------ gm%.

$$= 100 \times \text{observed value} / 14.5$$
$$= Y \%$$

➤ Oxygen carrying capacity of haemoglobin

$$100\% \text{ Hb} = 18.5 \text{ cc of oxygen}$$
$$Z = Y\% \times 18.5 / 100 \text{ Zcc of blood.}$$

> **Other various methods of haemoglobin content estimation**

1. Dare's method
2. Harden's method
3. Wintrobe's method
4. Halden's method
5. Tallquist's method
6. Gasometric method
7. Spectrophotometric oxyhaemoglobin method - A cyanmethaemoglobin method
8. Specific gravity method

> **Significance**

Physiological

RBC contains Hb which forms about 90% of dry weight of the cell.

RBC is called so, due to presence of red coloured haemoglobin. Reduced supply of haemoglobin to cell/ tissues leads to hypoxic condition, since haemoglobin carries oxygen to various cell/ tissues.

Clinical

Determination of haemoglobin content in blood will give an idea about whether the person is suffering from anaemia (a condition in which the oxygen carrying capacity of blood is reduced) or not. A person is said to be anemic if the Hb content falls below the normal range.

Hb content increases in the following conditions.

- High altitude
- Excessive sweating
- New born/ infants
- Diarrhoea

- Congenital heart diseases
- Emphysema
- Polycythemia vera- disorder of the bone marrow characterised by excessive production of RBCs.

Hb-content decreases in the following conditions.
- Pregnancy
- Anaemia

> **Anaemia (also spelled as anaemia)**

Anaemia is a condition in which the oxygen carrying capacity of blood is reduced. Anaemia predominantly occurs in female due to loss of blood during menstrual cycle and increased demand during pregnancy. The anemic condition can be treated by supplementation of iron containing food or medicine (folic acid).

> **Types of anaemia are listed below.**

1. **Iron deficiency anaemia :** Occurs due to inadequate absorption of iron, loss of iron, and increase demand of iron (during pregnancy) or reduced intake of iron. Menstruation and pregnancy are the two reasons why women are at high risk for iron deficiency anaemia.

2. **Megaloblastic anaemia :** Deficiency of folic acid or vitamin B_{12} (cyanocobalamin) resulting in abnormal production of RBCs (megaloblasts).

3. **Hemolytic anaemia :** It is caused due to premature rupture of plasma membrane of the RBCs. The haemoglobin enters into plasma and impairs the functioning of the kidneys.

4. **Pernicious anaemia :** It is caused due to insufficient hemopoiesis (a process of new blood cell formation) due to the inability of the stomach to produce intrinsic factor which is required for vitamin B_{12} absorption.

5. **Aplastic anaemia :** Occurs due to destruction of red bone marrow due to toxins, gamma radiation or some drugs.

6. **Thalassemia :** It is hereditary hemolytic anaemia due to deficient synthesis of haemoglobin.

EXERCISE

(a) What is haemoglobin (Hb)? Give the role of Hb.
(b) Give the normal values for haemoglobin.
(c) Give the role of HCl in Hb determination
(d) What is the importance of Hb in our body?
(e) What is anaemia? Enlist various types of anaemia?
(f) Discuss iron deficiency anaemia in brief.
(g) How can anaemia be treated?

❖❖❖

EXPERIMENT NO. 3

DETERMINATION OF THE NUMBER OF RBCS AND COLOUR INDEX OF BLOOD

(A) DETERMINATION OF NUMBER RED BLOOD CELLS

➤ **Aim**

To determine the number of red blood cells (RBCs) and colour index of blood.

➤ **Requirement**

Microscope, hemocytometer containing Neubauer's counting chamber, RBC pipette, sterile needle (22-24 gauge), coverslip, RBC diluting fluid.

➤ **Purpose of the hemocytometer**

The hemocytometer (also called counting chamber) is a specimen slide employed in determination of the concentration of blood cells [(hence it is called as "hemo" (blood) cyto (cells) meter]. It is frequently used to determine the concentration of blood cells but also the concentration of sperm cells in a sample. The cover glass, which is placed on the sample, does not simply float on the liquid, but is held in place at a specified height (usually 0.1mm). Additionally, a grid is fixed into the glass of the hemocytometer. This grid, an arrangement of squares of different sizes, allows for easy counting of cells.

➤ **Various diluting fluids**

(1) Hayem's fluid

Composition : Sodium chloride - 0.5 gm
Sodium sulphate - 2.5 gm
Mercuric chloride - 0.25 gm
Distilled water - 100 ml

(2) Dacie's fluid

Composition : Trisodium citrate - 3.13 gm
37% formalin - 1.0 ml
Distilled water - 100ml

➤ **Theory**

The red blood cells also called as erythrocytes, have circular, biconcave shape. They are non-nucleated cells and are red in colour. Their lifespan is of 120 days. Formation of RBCs in bone marrow (flexible tissue found in the interior of bones) is known as erythropoiesis. The main function of RBCs is to carry oxygen from the lungs to cells/ tissues of the body and CO_2 from cells/ tissues to lungs. The other functions of RBCs is to help maintain ionic and acid base balance, maintain viscosity of blood and various pigments like bilirubin and biliverdin which are derived from their disintegration.

➢ Normal ranges

In adults

Male : 4.5-6 millions/mm^3 of blood

Female : 4-5.5 millions/mm^3 of blood

Infants : 5-6.5 millions/mm^3 of blood

➢ Pathological Significance

The change in erythrocyte number is detected by haemoglobin determination rather than total RBC count. But in some clinical conditions like polycythemia, in which the total RBC is higher than normal or in pregnancy or anaemia where RBC count is less.

➢ Procedure

Using Neubauer's counting chamber

Neubauer's slide is a glass slide where two identical ruled areas separated by empty squares and having two elevated ridges on both the sides. Either of the ruled areas is used for counting the cells.

Figure 3.1 illustrates magnified divisions of square of 9 sq. mm (3 × 3mm) RBC chambers.

Red Blood Cells Count - Count the 5 small squares indicted by 'R'. Each of those squares contains 16 smaller squares. Use high power magnification for counting of cells (400 X).

White Blood Cell Count - Count the 4 large corner squares indicated by 'W'. Each of those squares contains 16 smaller squares the same size as one of the red cell squares. Use low power magnification (100X).

(a) The four corner squares of area 1 sq. mm each (1 mm × 1mm) are used for WBC count.

(b) The central sq. of area 1 sq. mm is sub divided into 25 sub squares. The four corner and one middle sub squares are used for RBC count(R).

$$R = 1/25 \text{ sq.mm}$$
$$= 0.04 \text{ sq.mm}$$

(c) Each R section is further sub divided into 16 squares for accurate cell measurement.

(d) Neubauer's slide has raised ridges on both sides of counting of 0.1 mm depth after keeping the cover slip in position. This space between ruled areas and cover slip will be filled with diluted fluid (blood).

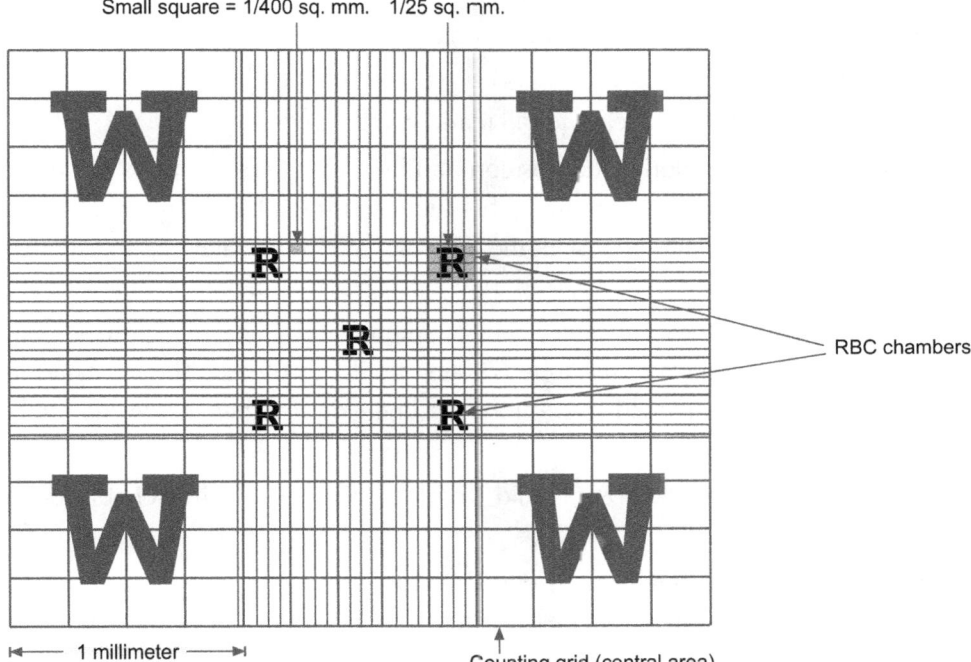

Figure 3.1 : Neubauer's counting chamber on a slide

➤ Preparation of slide

The RBCs (blood) with diluting fluid must be appropriately prepared before applying t to the hemocytometer.

Proper mixing : The mixture of blood and RBC dilution fluid should be a homogenous suspension. Cells that stick together in clumps are difficult to count as they are not evenly distributed. Therefore, proper mixing of sample blood and dilution fluid is essential for accurate measurements.

Appropriate concentration : The concentration of cells should neither be too high or too low. If the concentration is too high, then the cells overlap and are difficult to count. A low concentration of only a few cells per square results in a higher statistical error and it is then necessary to count more squares (which takes time). Suspensions that have a too high concentration should be diluted 1 :10, 1 :100 and 1 :1000. A 1 :10 dilution can be made by taking 1 part of the sample and mixing it with 9 parts water or saline of correct concentration to prevent bursting of the cells. The dilution part must later be considered when calculating the final concentration.

➢ Procedure

1. Take freshly prepared RBC diluting fluid in a watch glass.
2. Sterilse the skin on the finger with a cotton swab dipped in spirit and prick with sterilised needle.
3. Suck blood into the pipette up to 0.5 mark on the pipette.
4. Hold the pipette in horizontal position and by placing tip of pipette against index finger and blowing gently on the rubber tube, adjust the blood column, so that it is exactly on the 0.5 mark and suck the diluting fluid immediately up to 101 mark of the pipette.
5. Rotate the pipette for 2-3 minutes with its tip pressing against the left hand palm for mixing of the contents of the tube (diluting fluid and blood). The red bead in the bulb of the pipette should move from the one side to other during the mixing of blood cells.
6. Discard the first two drops of fluid from the pipette, which probably does not contain cells.
7. Placed tip of the pipette on the edged or ruled area and blow one-two drops of diluting blood (care should to be taken to prevent overflowing of the chamber.)
8. Place the charged chamber on the stage of microscope and adjust the microscope for observation under low power (10 X).
9. Focus the central square of the Neubauer's chamber and check the uniform distribution of RBCs.
10. Then focus the RBC square under high power objective (45 X). Count in the medium RBC square.
11. Counting of RBCs should start from small squares at upper left hand corner.
12. A cell that touches any of the triple lines that border the right side of RBC section should not be counted.
13. Count the cells in each small squares of RBC section and do it in all five RBC sections as shown in figure.
14. Calculate the total number of RBCs in blood.

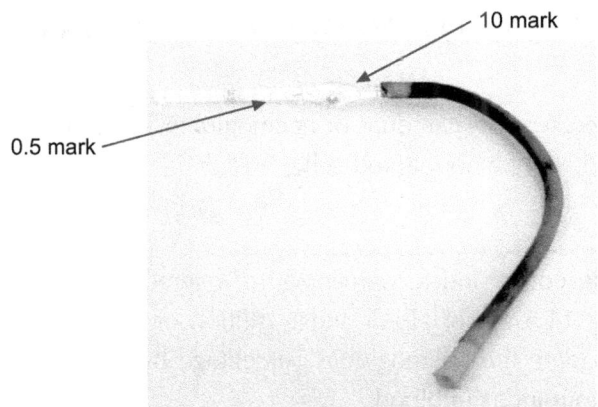

Figure 3.2 : RBC pipette

➤ Calculation

The RBC count has to be performed by mixing of blood with diluting fluid. Therefore, dilution correction factor to be calculated first

Therefore dilution correction factor,

= 0.5 part of blood in 100 parts of diluting fluid

i.e. = 0.5 to 100

= 1 : 200

Therefore dilution correction factor is 200 for 1 cumm.

Volume correction factor

Each RBC section has an area of 0.04 sq mm (1/25 = 0.04sq.mm) and depth of 0.1mm.

Area of 1 RBC Section × Depth of 1 RBC Section = Volume of 1 RBC Section

0.04 sqmm × 0.1mm = 0.004cumm

Total Volume of 5 RBC Sections = Volume of 5 RBC Sections.

= 0.004 × 5 = 0.02

Volume of correction factor (VCF) = $\frac{\text{Require volume}}{\text{Used volume}} = \frac{1 \text{ cu mm}}{0.02 \text{ cu mm}}$ = 50 cu mm

The Total RBC Count = No. of cells in 5 RBC sect × dilution factor × VCF

= X × 200 × 50

= Y cumm of Blood.

OR

RBCs count = Total No. cells in 5 RBC sections × 10,000 correction factor (200 × 50)

= million / mm^3 of blood

Result : The total RBC count of own blood was found to be ... million / mm^3 of blood

(B) DETERMINATION OF COLOUR INDEX OF BLOOD

Colour index represents the amount of haemoglobin in each red cell as compared to the haemoglobin content of a normal red cell.

➤ Calculation

To determine the colour index, percentage of haemoglobin and red blood cells are calculated by taking 14.5 gm of Hb/dl and 5 million of red cells/cumm as 100 %. The figure gained by dividing the haemoglobin percentage by the red blood cell percentage directly gives the colour index of blood.

The colour index is then calculated as follows

Hb content expressed as % of normal = x

Red blood cells expressed as % = y

Therefore, Colour Index = $\dfrac{x}{y}$

➤ Clinical Significance

RBC count decreases in pregnancy, during which there is high demand of haemoglobin for the foetus. Therefore, it is very essential to keep on checking haemoglobin as well as RBC count. Anaemia is due to loss of blood during menstruation also leads to decrease in RBC Count.

Colour index lesser than 1 indicates that the individual is suffering from anaemia.

EXERCISE

1. What are RBCs? Give the normal range of RBCs in male, female and infants?
2. Give the size and microscopic appearance of RBCs.
3. Enlist the functions of RBCs.
4. Give the significance of RBCs determination.
5. How are RBCs produced?
6. How are RBCs differentiated from other blood cells?
7. What is the colour index of blood?
8. Give the significance of colour index of blood.

EXPERIMENT NO. 4

STUDY OF OSMOTIC FRAGILITY OF RBCS

➤ Aim

To study the osmotic fragility of Red Blood Cells

➤ Requirements

Test tubes, distilled water, 1% w/v sodium chloride solution, dropper, test tube stand, anticoagulants (heparin) etc.

➤ Principle

Osmotic fragility of RBCs is the ability of red cells to rupture or hemolyse when they are exposed to hypotonic solution. When the RBCs are poured in sodium chloride solution (hypotonic), they swell till hemolysis occurs. The entry of hypotonic solution into the red cells puts pressure on the cell walls making them more fragile. Thus, fragility indicates the functional status of red cells.

➤ Procedure

1. Wash the test tubes and dry it and place in the stand having serial number from 1 to 12.
2. Prepare the solution with increasing hypotonicity by addition of number of drops of 1 % sodium chloride solution and distilled water as shown in table 4.1. The last tube contains only distilled water and no sodium chloride solution. Mix well all the tubes thoroughly.
3. Add a drop of blood containing anticoagulant.
4. Invert each tube carefully to mix the blood with solution and keep all the test tubes in stand for 30 minutes.
5. Observe the test tubes against a white background and note the tube for haemolysis (partial hemolysis is indicated by pink colour supernatant fluid with and red cells as sedimentation, complete hemolysis is indicated by clear, uniform pink solution

without red cells at the bottom of the tubes; and absence of hemolysis is indicated by straw coloured supernatant as shown in figure 4.1.

➢ Normal values

Osmotic fragility starts in the range of 0.45-0.50 and ends at the range of 0.30-0.35.

Table 4.1

Test tube no	1	2	3	4	5	6	7	8	9	10	11	12
Distilled water drops	3	9	10	11	12	13	14	15	16	17	18	25
1% Sodium chloride drops	22	16	15	14	13	12	11	10	9	8	7	0
% of solution obtained(conc)	0.88	0.64	0.60	0.56	0.52	0.48	0.44	0.40	0.36	0.32	0.28	0

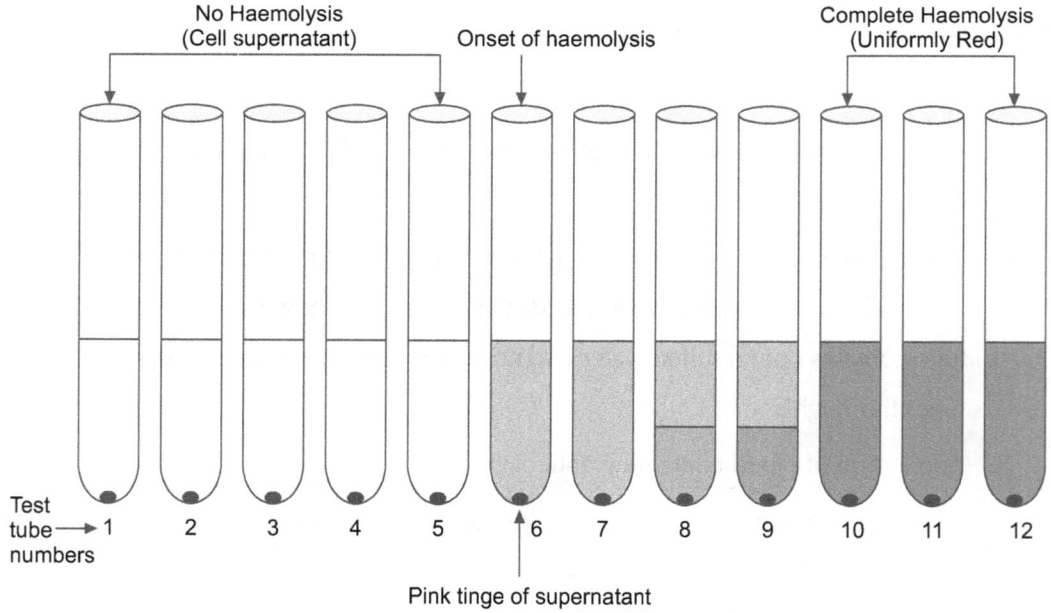

Figure 4.1. : Test tube showing complete hemolysis of red cells (tube no 10-12), no hemolysis (tube no 1-5) and partial hemolysis and onset of hemolysis

➤ Pathological Significance

The osmotic fragility is indicated by increase in haemolysis of RBCs. Osmotic fragility is related to cell membrane, shape of cell, surface area and volume. If the shape of cell is spherical, the haemolysis occurs at a faster rate.

The osmotic fragility of red cells decreases with reduction in haemolysis of RBCs indicating the increase in resistance of red cells to rupture.

In iron deficiency anaemia, the cells becomes very thin with lesser haemoglobin content, hence they swell faster before rupture occurs.

Osmotic fragility is increased in the following conditions

- Iron deficiency anaemia - characterised by low RBCs and is caused by insufficient dietary intake and absorption of iron, and/or iron loss from bleeding.
- Thalassemia
- Jaundice
- Sickle cell anaemia

Osmotic fragility is decreased in the following conditions

- Auto-haemolytic anaemia (spherocytosis) - a disease of the blood characterised by the production of red blood cells (RBCs) that are spherical rather than biconcave disk shaped.
- Hemolytic anaemia - characterised by abnormal breakdown of RBCs, in the blood vessels.

EXERCISE

1. What is osmotic fragility of red cells?
2. Give the principle of determination of osmotic fragility of red cells.

3. Give the normal range of osmotic fragility of red cells.
4. Give the pathological significance of osmotic fragility determination.
5. Enlist the conditions in which the osmotic fragility is increased.
6. Give the correlation of osmotic fragility and haemolysis.

EXPERIMENT NO. 5

DETERMINATION OF THE NUMBER OF WBCs IN BLOOD SAMPLE

➢ Aim

To determine the number of white blood cells (WBCs) in one's own blood sample.

➢ Requirements

Hemocytometer containing Neubauer's counting chamber, WBC pipette, sterile needle (gauge no 24), microscope, coverslip, WBC diluting fluid, spirit.

➢ Principle

The use of acetic acid solution with blood causes haemolysis of RBCs and accentuates nuclei of white cells. The WBC's can then be easily counted. The number of WBC/mm^3 of undiluted whole blood is calculated. Norma range of WBCs is 4500-10000/mm^3 of blood.

Theory : The white blood cells (WBCs) are also called as leukocytes. They are nucleated, actively amoeboid and do not contain haemoglobin and originate purely from extra vascular tissue. They contain proteins and various enzymes. Life span of WBCs is less than that of RBCs.

The types and subtypes of WBCs are given below.

1. Granulocytes   2. Agranulocytes

    A. Eosinophils   A. Lymphocytes

    B. Basophils   B. Monocytes

    C. Neutrophils

➢ Composition of diluting fluid

Glacial acetic acid - 1%

Gentian violet - 0.3%

Distilled Water - Q.S.

➢ Procedure

1. Take clean and dry apparatus. Use sterilised needle either having 22 or 24 gauge number. Prick the finger and allow blood drop to form on the fingertip spontaneously.

2. Take the pipette and suck the blood into the WBC pipette up to the 0.5 mark only (indicated on WBC pipette in figure 5.1).

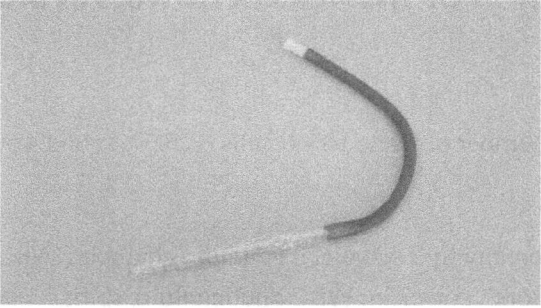

Figure 5.1 : WBC pipette

3. Wipe the tip of the pipette and maintain the blood level at the 0.5 mark by holding the pipette in a horizontal position.
4. Dip the pipette into the diluting fluid below the surface of the liquid.
5. Suck the WBC diluting fluid up to 11 marks. While the blub is being filled, tap the pipette with a finger to knock the bead below the surface of fluid in the bulb to prevent any bubble formation.
6. Maintain the level of the mixture at 11 marks by closing the tip of pipette with the index finger during removal of pipette from diluting fluid.
7. Hold the pipette horizontally and close the both ends of the WBC pipette, then gently mix the contents of the bulb.
8. After mixing, put the pipette in the horizontal position to prevent any loss of its content until the cell count is completed.
9. Discard the first 2 drops of fluid from the pipette as it does not contain the cells.
10. Charge the ruled area of the counting chamber taking care to prevent flooding.
11. Focus the microscope carefully and place the Neubauer's chamber on the stage of the microscope.
12. Look at the counting chamber from the side and by turning the coarse knob, lower the power objective (10 mm × 10 mm) until it is almost touching the cover glass.
13. Now while continuously looking through the eyepiece, slowly rotate the coarse adjustment towards yourself until you observe a faint line in the eyepiece. Adjust

the light with a mirror and diaphragm and use coarse adjustment back and fro until you get cells in good focus.

14. Count the number of cells.

➢ Calculation

Area of 4 WBC squares = 4 × 1 = 4mm^2

Volume of WBC squares = 4/10 mm^3

(1/10- 10 volumes of diluted blood in bulb contains 0.5 volume of blood and 9.5 volume of diluting fluid) hence, dilution is 1 in 20 (1 :20)

Cells in 4/10mm^3 volumes of diluted blood = x

Cells in 1 mm^3 volume of diluted blood = $\dfrac{10 \times x}{4}$

Cells in 1mm^3 volume of diluted fluid = $\dfrac{10 \times x \times 20}{4}$

= 50 × x

Therefore,

Total WBCs = Y/cu. mm of diluted blood.

➢ Results

The total white blood cells count of my own blood sample was found to be ...... /cu mm of blood.

➢ Clinical Significance

Leukocytosis : It is an increase in the number of WBCs above 10,500/mm^3. It is increased due to strenuous exercise, anesthesia, pregnancy surgery, urinary tract infection, bladder infection, kidney infection, asthma, and diabetic coma etc. High WBCs count in children may indicate whooping cough, bacterial or viral infection, measles, allergy or leukemia.

Leukopenia : It is an abnormal low level of WBCs below 4000 cells/ mm^3. This condition may arise due to radiation, shock, and various drugs especially anticancer agents. Low WBC count resulting from infection, make an individual more vulnerable to opportunistic infections.

EXERCISE

1. What are leukocytes (WBCs)? Enumerate on their size, shape and types.
2. Give the normal range of WBCs in a healthy adult.
3. Give the functions of WBCs in short.
4. What is the significance of WBC determination?
5. Give the composition of WBC dilution fluid.
6. Discuss the principle of WBCs determination.
7. Give the role of acetic acid in WBCs dilution fluid.
8. Define the term- Leukocytosis, and Leukopenia

EXPERIMENT NO. 6

DETERMINATION OF DIFFERENTIAL LEUKOCYTE COUNT OF BLOOD

➢ Aim

To determine the differential leukocyte count (DLC) of one's own blood.

➢ Requirement

Glass slide, microscope, staining dish, sterile disposable needle (gauge 24), cotton swab, rectified spirit, Leishman's stain or Wright's stain.

Leishman's stain consists of methyl alcohol, methylene blue and eosin.

➢ Principle

The polychromatic staining solution (Wright or Leishman's) contains methylene blue and eosin. Cytoplasm of cells stained with acidic dye is eosinophilic. When the acidic components i.e. nucleic acid within the nucleus is stained blue to purple colour with basic dye, the cells are known as basophilic. The cells which do not stain are known as neutrophils.

Theory

Leukocytes are nucleated, contain no haemoglobin and are classified as granular and agranular.

➢ Granular leukocytes

They are of three types as per their staining properties and appearance.

(a) Neutrophils : These cells do not stain either with acidic or basic stains, thus they are neutral and hence called neutrophils and appear pale lilac in colour. The nucleus of neutrophils has 2-5 lobes, connected by very thin strands of nuclear material. Neutrophils are also called as polymorphonuclear leukocytes due to their differently shaped nuclear lobe. Numbers increase during inflammatory conditions (infections) as defense mechanism and decrease during radiation exposure and deficiency of vitamin B_{12}. Normal range is 50-70 %.

(b) Eosinophils : These cells are eosin loving and stain red-orange with acidic dye (red), hence called eosinophils. Granules of eosinophils are large and uniform in size. The granules do not cover the nucleus, having two lobes connected with either thin or thick strand of nuclear materials. Eosinophil counts increase in cases asthma, hay fever (allergic rhinitis or common cold) and decrease in cases of burns and acute infection. Normal range is 2-3 %.

(c) Basophils : The round, variable-sized granules stain blue-purple with basic dyes. They are very small in number with normal value ranges from 0-1 %. Basophils increase during incidences of asthma, hay fever and decreases during pregnancy, ovulation, stress and hypothyroidism.

➢ Agranular leukocytes

These cells have cytoplasmic granules, which are invisible under light microscope due to their poor staining properties and are small in size.

(a) Monocytes : Monocytes have kidney or horseshoe shaped nucleus and the cytoplasm appears blue gray (azurophilic granule) and foamy. Monocytes upon differentiation are converted into macrophages (large eaters) in tissue after their migration. Monocytes increase during tuberculosis, typhoid, monocytic infection, leukaemia and decrease in bone marrow suppression. The normal value of monocytes ranges from 2-8 %.

(b) Lymphocytes : Lymphocytes have round nucleus and cytoplasm that stains sky-blue and forms a rim around the nucleus. Depending upon the size of the cell and part of nucleus occupying the cytoplasm, they are further classified as small lymphocytes (7.5 μ with large nucleus) and large lymphocytes (12-14 μ size with small nucleus). The normal value of lymphocytes ranges from 20-45%. Lymphocytes increase when a person is suffering from leukemia, asthma and decreases in immunosuppression.

➢ Procedure

1. Clean the tip of the middle finger with spirit (70% alcohol) and prick the finger with the help of a sterile needle.
2. Place a drop of blood on one end of slide (about 1cm from end). Take care not to touch the finger with the slide.
3. Place the specimen slide on the flat surface of the table and take another slide (which acts as a spreader) and place it on specimen slide at an angle of 30^0-40^0C.
4. Draw the spreader back until it touches the blood drop; let the blood run along the edge of the spreader. Drag the spreader smoothly along the entire length of the specimen slide to get a uniform smear.
5. Allow the smear to dry for up to 5-10 min.
6. Add sufficient quantity of stain on the smear with the help of a dropper, wait for 1min and then add 20-30 drops of buffer solution, mix and allow it to stand for 10min.

7. Pour water on the smear to flush off the excess staining solution and allow the slide to dry.

8. Add a drop of cedar wood oil (immersion oil) on the smear and then bring the oil immersion objective in position and lower the nosepiece such that the end of the objective touches the drop of oil and then focus the cell.

9. Counting of differential leukocytes should begin from one end as shown in the following figure.

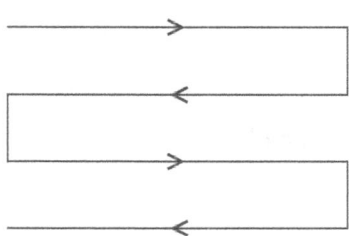

10. Count a minimum of 100 WBCs.

11. Determine and calculate the differentiate leukocyte in percentage.

➤ Observation

Different leukocytes are divided into five groups and the number of lines are marked on the observation note book.

Neutrophils	⫽ ⫽ ⫽ ⫽ ⫽ ...... ⫽	= 55 cells
Eosinophils	|||	= 3 cells
Basophils	0	= 0 cells
Lymphocytes	⫽ ⫽ ...... ⫽	= 42 cells
Monocyte	||	= 2 cells
		100 cells

10 × 10 – (Measurement of differential leukocytes in following fashion

N	L	L	L	L	N	L	L	L	N
L	N	M	N	N	L	N	M	N	L
L	M	N	E	L	N	M	N	N	N
N	N	N	N	N	L	N	L	L	L
L	N	L	N	N	M	N	L	N	N

N	N	N	L	N	L	L	E	L	L
N	L	L	N	L	N	N	L	N	N
N	N	N	M	N	L	L	N	L	L
L	L	N	N	N	N	L	L	N	L
M	N	L	L	N	L	N	E	L	N

N - Neutrophils, E - Eosinophils, B - Basophils, L - Lymphocytes, M - Monocytes

➤ Result

The differential leukocyte count of my blood sample was found to be ...... %

Hence, the DLC of my blood sample is normal/abnormal.

➤ Inference

If DLC is abnormal, then eosinophilia or neutropenia to be noted.

➤ Clinical Significance

An increase in the number of circulating WBCs usually indicates inflammation or infection. The DLC count is to detect infection or inflammation, determine the effects of possible poisoning by chemicals, drugs, monitor various blood disorder/diseases (eg. eosinophilia, leukemia) and effects of chemotherapy or determination of allergic reaction, parasitic infections.

EXERCISE

1. What is differential leukocyte count?
2. Give the normal values of DLC.
3. Give the composition and role of Leishman's stain for DLC determination.
4. Give the classification of leukocytes with examples.
5. Give the functions of neutrophils, eosinophils and basophils.
6. Give the principle involved in the determination of DLC counts
7. What is the significance of determination of DLC?
8. Enlist various disorders in which DLC is abnormal.

EXPERIMENT NO. 7

DETERMINATION OF PLATELET COUNT OF BLOOD

➢ **Aim**

To determine the platelet count of one's own blood sample.

➢ **Requirements**

Neubauer's chamber, haemocytometer with RBC pipette, microscope, petri dish, sterile needle (24gauze), filter paper, and Rees-Ecker reagent.

➢ **The composition of Rees-Ecker regent**

Sodium chloride	3.8 g
Formalin	0.22 ml
Brilliant cresyl blue	0.05 g
Deionised water	q.s. 100 ml

➢ **Principle**

The principle of platelet count by Rees-Ecker method involves addition of Brilliant cresyl blue to whole blood containing anticoagulant (EDTA) that results in appearance of platelets as light blue bodies without affecting RBCs.

➢ **Theory**

Platelets also known as thrombocytes, are differentiated from hemopoietic stem cells. They are the cytoplasmic fragments of megakaryocytes (myeloid stem cells form megakaryoblasts and then into megakaryocytes). Aggregation of platelets prevents haemorrhage (excessive bleeding) from the vessels.

➢ **Normal platelets count**

150000-450000 per μl of blood (or per mm^3 of blood)

➢ **Procedure**

1. Clean and dry the pipette and Neubauer's chamber before starting the experiment.
2. Puncture the figure tip with needle and allow the blood to flow easily, suck the blood in RBC pipette up to 0.5 mark.

3. Immediately, dilute the blood with Rees-Ecker fluid up to 101 mark of RBC pipette.
4. Shake the pipette for 60 seconds for complete mixing.
5. Discard first 2-3 drops of mixture, and then pour the drop on Neubauer's chamber to charge it.
6. Place a cover of a Petri dish on the chamber lined with moist filter paper for 15 minutes to allow the platelets to settle down.
7. After 15 minutes, observe the platelets (they appear as oval, bluish and round with 2-3 µm diameter) under high power objective.
8. Count the platelets in all the 25 medium squares of RBC squares i.e. 1 mm² or 1/10 mm.cu.
9. Note the count in the squares on the paper.

➢ Calculation

Platelets count per mm³ of blood

$$= \frac{\text{Number of platelets counted} \times \text{dilution}}{\text{Volume of fluid}}$$

Dilution factor = 200 (as per WBC experiment)

Volume of fluid (1 mm²) = 1 × 1/10

= 1 × 0.1

= 0.1 µl mm³

Therefore, platelets count per mm³ of blood

= Number of platelets mm³ × 200/0.1

= Number of platelets counted × 2000

Result: The platelets count of my own blood found to be .... cells per mm³ of blood.

Necessary precaution to be taken before the start of the experiment

1. The glassware should be thoroughly clean and dry or otherwise platelets might adhere on the glass.
2. The diluting fluid should be filtered before use for removal of any stained particles.

3. The blood should be diluted and mixed immediately with diluting fluid so as to avoid formation of clumps (aggregation of platelets).

Platelets count decreases due to

- HELLP syndrome (Hemolysis, Elevated Liver enzymes and Low Platelet count) observed during pregnancy.
- Hemolytic uremic syndrome- characterised by hemolytic anaemia, acute kidney failure, and a low platelet count, elevated lactate dehydrogenase, associated with abdominal pain, proteinuria, confusion, fatigue, nausea, vomiting and diarrhea.
- Chemotherapy.
- Dengue- an infectious tropical disease caused by the dengue virus and is characterised by low platelet count (below 100000 per µl of blood), high grade fever (body temperature more than 39 °C), headache, muscle and joint pains, and a characteristic skin rash

Platelets count increases due to

- Polycythemia vera (is a myeloproliferative blood disorder in which the bone marrow makes too many red blood cells),
- Chronic leukemia,
- Iron deficiency anaemia
- Bacterial or viral infection

> **Clinical Significance**

Thrombocytosis or thrombocythemia is a condition in which platelets count increases greater than the normal value

Thrombocytopenia is the condition in which platelets count decreases below the normal values. The impaired platelets production is the main reason for thrombocytopenia.

If the platelets number is too low it may result in haemorrhage, continuous bleeding etc, whereas, if platelets are too high, it results in stroke, myocardial infarction and pulmonary embolism (blockage of the main artery of lung or its branches).

EXERCISE

1. Give the composition of Rees-Ecker regent.
2. What are platelets? Give the normal range of platelet count.
3. Give the principle involved in determination of platelets count.
4. Define the term thrombocytosis and thrombocytopenia
5. Why do the platelet count increase or decrease?
6. Enlist various disorders in which platelet count increases or decreases.

EXPERIMENT NO. 8

DETERMINATION OF RETICULOCYTE COUNT OF BLOOD

> ## Aim

To determine the normal reticulocyte count of one's own blood sample

> ## Requirements

Microscope, glass slides, watch glass, filter paper, sterile needle (24 gauze) and Brilliant cresyl blue stain.

> ## The composition of Brilliant cresyl blue stain

Dissolve 1.0 grams of brilliant cresyl blue in 99 ml of 0.85 per cent sodium chloride.

Instead of Brilliant cresyl blue stain, other stains like methylene blue solution can be employed. It is prepared by adding 0.5 grams of new methylene blue, 1.4 grams of potassium oxalate, and 0.8 grams of sodium chloride in distilled water (q.s.) to produce 100 ml of the stain.

Filter the solution before use.

> ## Principle

The RNA content of reticulocytes is determined by staining living cells with supravital stain (Brilliant cresyl blue stain). In this, blood cells are mixed with stain as opposed to DLC where the smear is made before staining.

> ## Theory

In the normal blood, 0.5-1.5 % of the RBCs contains fine reticulum within cytoplasm. The reticulocytes are the immature RBCs that develop and mature in the red bone marrow and circulate into blood for short time before their maturation. Reticulocytes are violet fragment granules arranged in a network without nucleus. Reticulocytes serve as an index of the activity of the bone marrow in blood regeneration.

> ## Normal reticulocytes count

Adult :   0.5-1.5 %

New born :   3-6 %

➤ Procedure

1. Clean and dry the glass slides and pour a drop of stain on it.
2. Prick the figure with needle and allow blood drop to form.
3. Add a drop of blood onto the stain; mix the blood gently with the blunt edge of a slide.
4. Cover the glass slide with a watch glass lined with moist filter paper for about 15 minutes.
5. After 15 minutes, place the edge of spreader on the mixture, transfer a part of mixture to the spreader to another slide to make thin smear (at least 2- 3 smears should be prepared) and then allow to dry.
6. Focus the low power objective initially to locate a thin portion of the smear.
7. Then change the low power objective to oil immersion objective so that nearly about 100-150 red cells are clearly visible.
8. Distinguish between the red cells (they appear pale blue) and reticulocytes (reticulocytes are identified as violet fragment granules arranged in network).
9. Count both the cells i.e. reticulocytes and red cells in each field, minimum 1000 cells in 10 fields and estimate as

Field no	Reticulocytes (numbers)-A	Red blood cells (numbers)-B	Total cells (A+B)
:			
:			
:			
:			
:			
15			

➤ Calculation

$$\text{Reticulocytes count} = \frac{\text{Number of reticulocytes}}{\text{Total number of cells observed}}$$

If, total number of reticulocytes and number of RBCs are 1500, and reticulocytes observed are 75, then

$$\text{Reticulocytes count} = \frac{75 \times 100}{1500}$$

$$= 0.5\%$$

Result: The reticulocytes count of my own blood was found to be ---------- %.

➤ Pathological significance

The number of reticulocytes in circulation ensures the normal functioning of bone marrow. The reticulocytes count is determined to check whether the individual is healthy and does not suffer from anaemia during the drug treatment. During vitamin B_{12} treatment in pernicious anaemia, the reticulocytes count increase which indicates that the treatment is satisfactory.

Reticulocytosis - is the increase in reticulocyte count above normal values

Reticulocytopenia or "aplastic crisis" is an abnormal decrease of reticulocytes in the body.

The reticulocytes increase under cases of

- Hemolytic anaemia
- Acute haemorrhage
- Increase in bone marrow cell production

The reticulocytes decrease under conditions of

- Aplastic anaemia - is the inability of the stem cells to produce the mature blood cells due to damage of stem cells.
- Hypopituitarism (decreased secretion of hormones from pituitary gland)
- Myxedema or hypothyroidism

EXERCISE

1. What are reticulocytes? Mention their normal values.
2. Give the composition of Brilliant cresyl blue stain.
3. Give the principle involved in estimation of reticulocytes count.
4. Enlist the disorders in which reticulocytes count increases or decreases

EXPERIMENT NO. 9

DETERMINATION OF ARNETH COUNT OF BLOOD

➤ Aim

To find out the Arneth count of one's own blood.

➤ Requirement

Glass slide, microscope, staining dish, sterile disposable needle (gauge 24), cotton swab, rectified spirit, Leishman's stain

➤ Principle

Arneth index or count explains the nucleus of a type of a neutrophil, a type of white blood cell used to detect disease/disorder. The neutrophils are grouped according to the lobes of their nuclei and their percentage is determined.

➤ Theory

On the basis of the number of lobes of the nucleus, neutrophils is grouped into various stages. Joseph Arneth, a German physiologist classified the neutrophils into various stages based on their degree of maturity and appearance of lobes (figures 9.1), i.e.

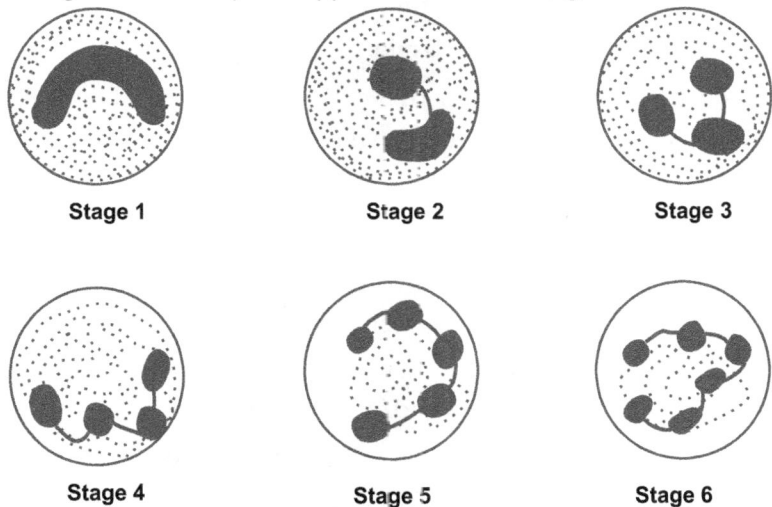

Figure 9.1 : Stages of neutrophil development

Stage 1 - the unilobe or stab as there is a single rod shaped nucleus, lobes are in thin strands and nucleus is 'U'shaped.

Stage 2 - the two lobes of the nucleus are connected by a thin strand.

Stage 3 - the three lobes of the nucleus are connected by a thin strand.

Stage 4 - the four lobes of the nucleus are connected by a thin strand.

Stage 5 - the five lobes of the nucleus are connected by a thin strand.

Stage 6 - the six lobes of the nucleus are connected by a thin strand.

The size of the neutrophils or the number of granules present in it is taken for the calculation when there is difficulty in staging the nucleus.

➢ **Procedure**
1. Clean the tip of the middle finger with spirit (70% alcohol) and prick the finger with the help of a sterile needle.
2. Place a drop of blood on one end of the slide. Take care not to touch the tip of the finger with the slide.
3. Place the specimen slide on the flat surface of the table and take another slide (which acts as a spreader) and place it on the specimen slide at an angle of 30^0-40^0C.
4. Draw the spreader back until it touches the blood drop, let the blood run along the edge of the spreader and drag the spreader smoothly along the entire length of the specimen slide to get a uniform smear.
5. Allow the smear to dry up for 5-10 min.
6. Add adequate quantity of stain (5-10 drops) to the smear with the help of a dropper and wait for 1 min and then add 20-30 drops of buffer solution, mix and allow it to stand for 10 min.
7. Pour water on the smear to flush off the excess staining solution and allow the slide to dry.
8. Place a drop of cedar wood oil (immersion oil) on the smear. Bring the oil or immersion objective in position such that the lower end of the objective touches the drop of oil . Adjust the object and focus the cell.
9. Count the lobes of neutrophils as stage 1, stage 2, stage 3, stage 4, stage 5, and stage 6 etc as per their appearance. Count at least 100 neutrophils as done in DLC experiment,
10. Calculate the percentage of neutrophils (if number of neutrophils in stage 1 is 10-, then it is 10 %; stage 2- neutrophils 29 then it is 29 % etc.) Plot a graph of neutrophil (%) against the stages of neutrophils (figure 9.2)

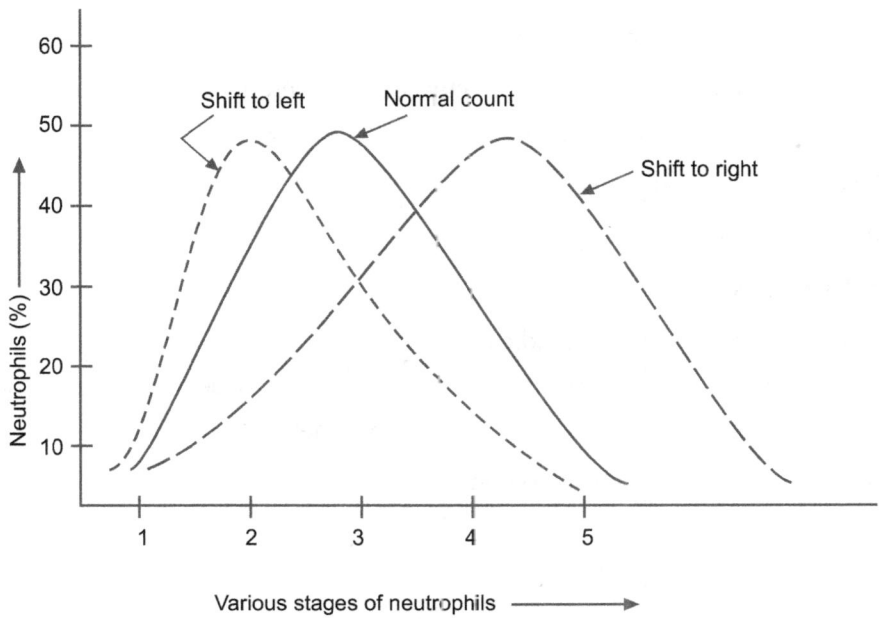

Figure 9.2 : Arenth curve

➢ **Normal count**

Stage 1 : 3-10 %

Stage 2 : 20-30 %

Stage 3 : 40-50 %

Stage 4 : 10-15 %

Stage 5 : 2-4 %

Stage 6 : 0-2 %

Pathological significance : The Arneth count is used to determine the number of young and old neutrophils in the blood sample. As the younger neutrophils take part in defense system and are involved in phagocytosis during infection or injury, the neutrophil concentration is higher in the injured area or infectious site. The Arneth count reveals the active functioning of bone marrow as it is the site of neutrophils production.

Shift to left : The shift to left indicates when there are more than 50 % neutrophils in stage 1 and stage 2, as there is higher production from bone marrow. It is also known as regenerative shift.

In the following conditions the shift to left occurs-

- **Pyogenic infection-** infection characterised by severe local inflammation, with pus formation at the site of infection.
- **Haemorrhagic conditions.**
- **Bacterial infection.**
- **Tuberculosis**

Shift to right : The shift to right indicates when there are more than 20 % neutrophils in stage 4 and 5, and in this the older cells are found due to decrease in production of neutrophils by bone marrow and shift is known as degenerative shift.

In the following conditions, the shift to right occurs-

- **Anaemia**
- **Uremia**
- **Septicemia**

EXERCISE

1. What is Arneth count?
2. Give the principle of Arneth count.
3. Give the normal Arneth count.
4. Discuss the clinical significance of Arneth count.

EXPERIMENT NO. 10

DETERMINATION OF ERYTHROCYTE SEDIMENTATION RATE

➢ Aim

To determine the erythrocyte sedimentation rate (ESR) of own blood.

➢ Requirements

Westergren pipette (Westergren method) or Wintrobe tube (Wintrobe method), rack, pipette, cotton swab, spirit, sterile needle (24 gauge).

➢ Principle

Blood containing anticoagulant is taken in Wintrobe pipette and kept as it is in vertical position. The level of the column of Wintrobe pipette is noted in the beginning (0 hr) and after 1, 2 hrs. The distance (mm) the column moves is noted as ESR (mm/h)

➢ Theory

Sedimentation of red cells occurs when blood is mixed with EDTA (anticoagulant) and allowed to settle. The reaction at which the red cells settle down is known as ESR. This is to be differentiated from haematocrit (PCV) in which pack cell volume is determined by the use of centrifugation while the column of red cells settle by gravity.

Sedimentation of red cells occurs due to piling up formation (Rouleaux) which appears as a stack of coins. Red cells get heavier due to formation of rouleaux and if the number of rouleaux is high, sedimentation of cells is faster

➢ Wintrobe method

Normal values

Male - 0 - 9 mm/h

Female - 0 - 20 mm/h

➢ Procedure

1. Take blood (with EDTA as anticoagulant) in pipette, mix thoroughly by inversion or swirling for 2 minutes.

2. Fill up the Wintrobe tube up to the mark with blood. While filling up blood, care has to be taken to prevent any bubble formation inside the Wintrobe tube.
3. Place the Wintrobe tube in Wintrobe rack at vertical position and note the time.
4. Note the reading of the erythrocyte column at the end of 1 hr and express the ESR as mm/hr.

Result : The ESR of my own blood sample was found to be -------mm/hr.

> ## Clinical Significance

The ESR is a non specific test to detect inflammatory conditions and found to increase in diseases or disorders associated with inflammation. An increase in plasma fibrinogen as observed in pneumonia or increase in globulin in tuberculosis or rheumatoid arthritis. ESR also increases in carcinoma/leukemia. ESR determination is significant to define one of the several possible adverse prognostic factors in the staging of Hodgkin's lymphoma. Therefore, the ESR is the index of inflammatory process in the body.

EXERCISE

1. What is ESR? Differentiate ESR from hematocrit.
2. Give the methods for ESR determination.
3. Give the clinical significance of ESR.

EXPERIMENT NO. 11

DETERMINATION OF BLOOD GROUP

➢ Aim

To determine the blood group of one's own blood sample.

➢ Requirements

Glass slide or slide with 3-4 cavities (cavity slide), sterile needle, spirit, antiserum A (blue), B (yellow), C (colourless).

➢ Principle

The procedure used with antisera is based on the principal of agglutination (clumping of RBC in the presence of antibody). Normal human red cells possessing antigens will clump in the presence of corresponding antibody (agglutination occurs).

➢ Theory

ABO blood group is based on two glycolipids namely antigen A and antigen B. Persons with antigen A on their RBCs fall under blood group A. those with B antigen on their RBCs have blood group B and those who have both A and B antigens on their RBCs fall under blood group AB. Individuals who possess neither A or B antigens fall under blood group O and is known as universal donor, who can donate blood to any person (figure 11.1).

➢ Rh blood group

The Rh group is so named because the antigen was first discovered in the blood of Rhesus monkey. Individual whose RBCs have Rh antigens are denoted as Rh⁺ (positive) and those who do not possess Rh antigens are denoted as Rh negative.

➢ Procedure

1. Clean and dry the cavity slide
2. Mark the cavities of the slide as A, B, D.
3. Place a drop of anti A, anti B and anti D respectively in the cavity.
4. Sterilise finger tip with a cotton swab dipped in spirit and prick the finger using a sterilised needle.

5. Add 1-2 drops of blood in each depression and mix it immediately with the help of a sealed glass capillary or by gentle shaking of cavity slide on plain horizontal surface.
6. Observe agglutination formation in each depression.
7. Note the observation and carefully identify the particular blood group (as shown in figure 11.2).

Antigen-A serum	Antigen-B serum	Agglutination in RBC	Blood group
Agglutination (+)	No agglutination (-)	A	A
No agglutination (-)	Agglutination (+)	B	B
Agglutination (+)	Agglutination (+)	AB	AB
No agglutination (-)	No agglutination (-)	Nil	O

Agglutination is the formation of grainy clumps and RBC suspended in clear solution.

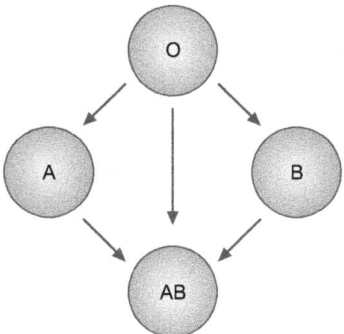

Figure 11.1 : Red blood cell compatibility (Individual with blood group can be universal donor i.e. can donate blood to an individual with any blood group)

➤ Significance

It is very important to carefully cross match or screen the blood group before transfusion to prevent the hemolysis. The consequences likely to develop due to the mismatched blood group transfusion include, anaphylactic reaction (characterised by bronchoconstriction, edema), jaundice, renal failure due because of damage of renal tubules with haemoglobin, and cardiac complications (due to high potassium level in blood). Acute haemolytic transfusion reaction occurs due to rapid destruction of the donor RBCs by host antibodies (IgG, IgM). This is usually seen when an individual having group A and donates blood to a patient with blood group O.

> **Erythroblastosis fetalis**

Erythroblastosis fetalis occurs due to Rh incompatibility. When an Rh negative mother carries Rh positive foetus, usually no reactions occur in first pregnancy, however, if mother has received transfusion of Rh positive blood earlier, reaction may occur during first pregnancy. A small amount of blood leakage into the maternal circulation at the time of delivery induces anti-Rh agglutins in mother. In subsequent pregnancies, the mother's agglutinin crosses the placenta of the foetus and causes hemolysis in the foetus and fetus may die in the uterus or may have anaemia, jaundice and edema if the foetus is born alive. There is presence of erythroblasts in the blood.

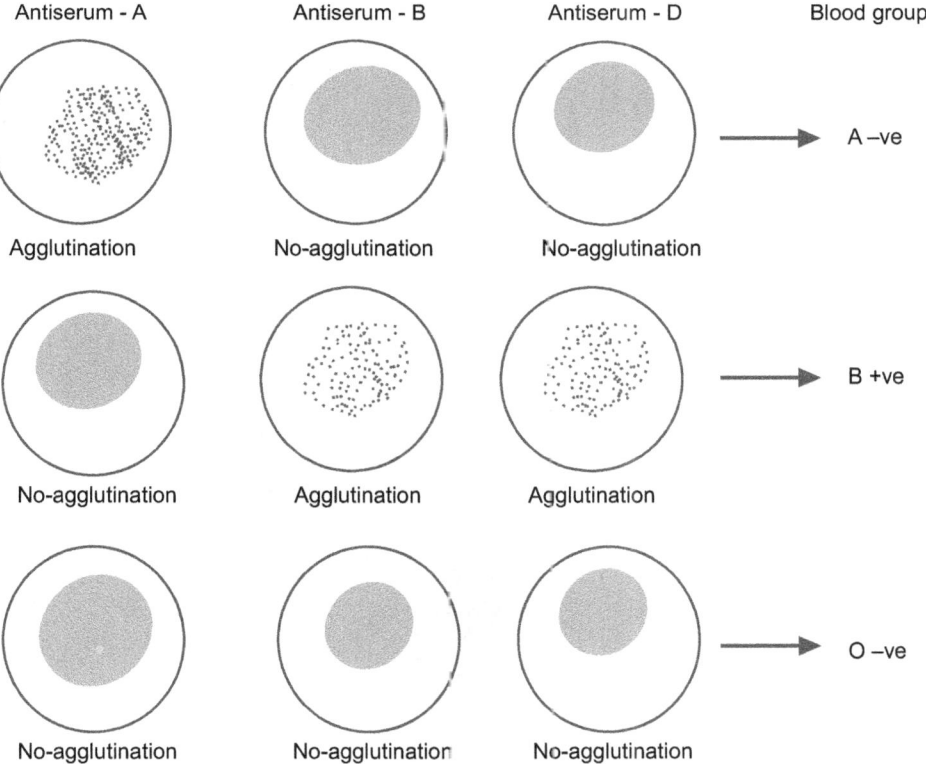

Figure 11.2 : Types of Blood Groups

EXERCISE

1. Give the significance of blood group determination
2. What is the basis of blood group determination?
3. Which blood groups are known as universal receiver and donor respectively? Justify
4. What is agglutination?
5. What is Rh system?
6. How does erythroblastosis fetalis develop?

EXPERIMENT NO. 12

DETERMINATION OF HEMATOCRIT CONTENT OF BLOOD

➢ Aim

To determine the hematocrit content of one's own blood sample.

➢ Requirements

Centrifuge machine (2300g), Wintrobe tube having 110 mm long, 3 mm internal diameter and with 0-10 cm graduated mark.

The scale 0-10 from above is used for ESR determination, whereas below 0-10 is used for hematocrit determination. Pasture pipette- 22cm long tube with long nozzle about 13cm in length.

Blood sample- blood sample with anticoagulant (EDTA).

➢ Principle

Wintrobe tube containing blood mixed with anticoagulant to be filled up to the desired mark and centrifuged for a prescribed time. The packed cell volume is read directly from the graduation mark on the tube.

➢ Theory

Hematocrit involves blood separation, and a measure of the percentage of volume of packed red cells. These packed red cells are called hematocrit and termed as Packed Cell Volume (PCV).

➢ Procedure

1. Mix the blood with anticoagulant (EDTA) and fill in Wintrobe tube with the help of Pasteur pipette up to 10cm (100%)

2. Place the Wintrobe tube in the centrifuge cups, taking care to see that the centrifuge is balanced. Place the wintrobe tubes in opposite cups and place the water filled Wintrobe tubes in the empty slots for balancing.

3. Turn on the centrifuge machine and adjust slowly upto the desired speed (3300rpm for 30min)

4. After 30min, switch off the centrifuge and allow it to stop completely before removing the Wintrobe tubes. Read the packed cell volume directly off the graduation

> **Normal values**

Adult – 46% (40-50%)

Female – (37-47%)

> **Pathological significance**

Hematocrit is an index of Hb content of red blood cells. Therefore, it is used to detect polycythemia (increased RBC) or anaemia (decrease Hb/ RBC). It is also used for determination of blood indices, MCV- mean capsular volume, and MCHC- mean capsular haemoglobin concentration. Hematocrit is also important in determination of blood viscosity. This increases the peripheral resistance which results in decreased cardiac output due to increase afterload on the heart.

Result : The hematocrit content of my own blood was found to be …… %.

EXERCISE

1. What is hematocrit?
2. Give the significance of hematocrit determination.
3. What is packed cell volume (PCV) and mean corpuscle volume (MCV)?
4. How is hematocrit related to anaemia?
5. Give the normal range of hematocrit?

❖❖❖

EXPERIMENT NO. 13

DETERMINATION OF BLEEDING TIME AND CLOTTING TIME OF BLOOD

> **Aim**

To determine the bleeding time and clotting time of one's own blood.

> **Requirements**

Sterile needle (22-24 gauge), spirit, stopwatch, glass capillary tubes, filter paper

> **Principle**

Bleeding Time: Bleeding time depends on the effectiveness of vasoconstriction and platelet plug formation. It is defined as the time from onset of bleeding till the stoppage of bleeding. Length of time needed for bleeding to cease is noted after deep skin puncture. It determines the function of platelets and integrity of the capillaries.

Clotting Time: Clotting time is the length of time it takes for the blood to clot and is detected by the appearance of fibrin string.

> **Theory**

Bleeding and clotting times are determined for assessing the integrity of haemostatic mechanism. The process of cease of blood flow is termed as haemostasis resulting due to either alone or in combination of process of vasoconstriction, platelet plug formation and coagulation of blood.

> **Procedure**

Estimation of Bleeding Time : By Duke's Method

1. Clean the finger tip with spirit or alcohol and make a deep puncture with the help of sterile needle.
2. Start the stop watch immediately and count the time.
3. Place a drop of blood on the filter paper after every 30 seconds.
4. Note the time of stoppage of blood
5. This gives the bleeding time

> **Observation :**

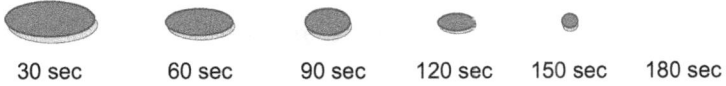

30 sec   60 sec   90 sec   120 sec   150 sec   180 sec

The normal range of bleeding time by Duke's method is 2-5 minutes

Results : The bleeding time of my own blood was found to be .... minutes

Estimation of Clotting Time : By capillary tube method

1. Follow the steps of bleeding time estimation upto step 2.

2. Wipe off the first drop of blood and allow the next drop of blood to flow into the capillary tube by introducing one end of the tube into the drop and holding the other end at lower level.

3. Hold the capillary tube between the palms.

4. Wait for 2min, and then break off the capillary tube 1-2 cm from one side every 30 sec and observe the formation of fibrin thread (insoluble protein fibres).

5. Note the time at which fibrin is formed that indicates the clotting time of blood.

➢ **Observation**

Normal values : The normal range of clotting time by capillary tube method is 2-8 minutes.

➢ **Clinical Significance**

Bleeding time : Increased bleeding time may due to a variety of blood disorders, thrombocytopenia, haemophilia etc. Bleeding time ensures normal functioning of platelets.

Aspirin and other prostaglandin synthase inhibitors can prolong bleeding time significantly. Anticoagulants like warfarin and heparin have major effects on coagulation factors, and increase bleeding time.

Clotting time : Clotting time is found to increase in various pathophysiological conditions mainly in haemophilia, heat stroke, toxic effects of venom, clotting factor deficiency (Factor II, V and XI).

EXERCISE

1. What is bleeding time? Give significance of its estimation.

2. Give the normal range of bleeding time and clotting time.

3. What is the significance of clotting time?

4. Mention the disorders in which bleeding time and clotting time is prolonged.

EXPERIMENT NO. 14

DETERMINATION OF BLOOD PRESSURE

➢ **Aim**

To determine one's own blood pressure (BP)

➢ **Requirements**

Sphygmomanometer, stethoscope (figure 14.1)

➢ **Principle**

Blood pressure is the hydrostatic pressure exerted by blood on the walls of blood vessels. It is determined by cardiac output, blood volume, and vascular resistance. Sphygmomanometer is an instrument exclusively used for determination of blood pressure in humans. Blood pressure is the pressure in arteries produced by the left ventricle at the time of contraction (systole) and the pressure remaining in the arteries produced by the ventricle is in a state of relaxation (diastole).

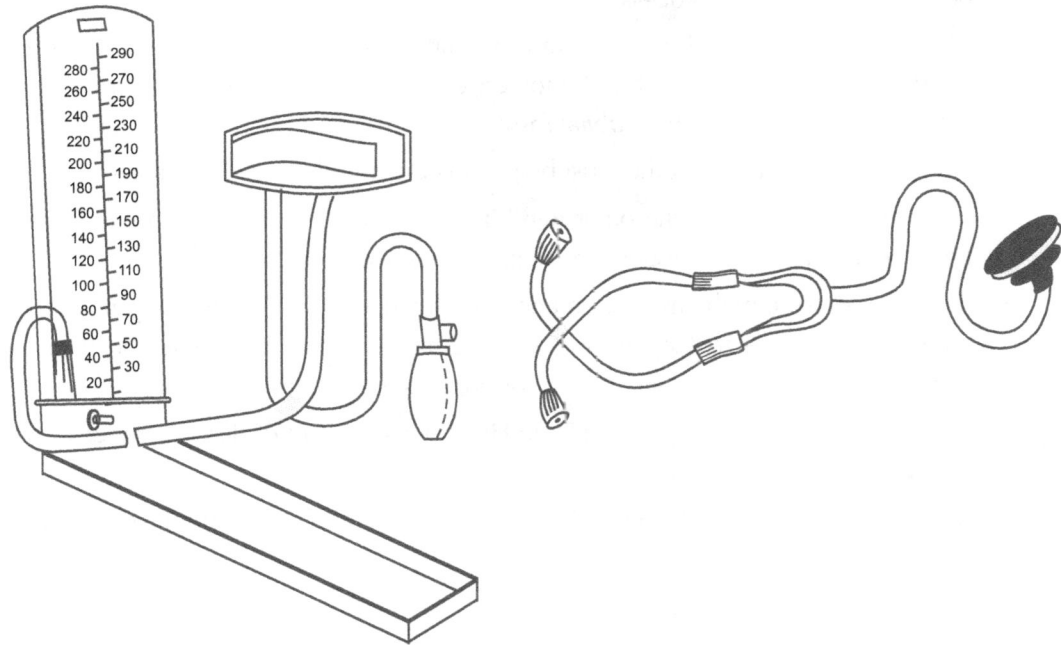

Figure 14.1 : Sphygmomanometer and stethoscope

By this technique, wrap the cuff around the arm, and then inflate (increase the air through the air pump) till the pressure in the cuff overcomes the arterial pressure, artery is compressed, so that blood flow through arteries ceases. Then place the stethoscope below the cuff, slowly release the pressure by deflating the cuff. When the cuff is deflated enough to allow the blood to flow, the first sound is heard through the stethoscope. This sound corresponds to systolic pressure (pressure exerted during ventricular contraction); on continued deflation of cuff (release of air), suddenly the sound becomes faint and then corresponds to diastolic pressure (pressure exerted by the blood on arteries during ventricular relaxation. Appearance of sound during systole and diastole are called as Korotkoff sound (named after Dr. Nikolai Korotkoff, a Russian physician who described them in 1905).

The difference between systolic and diastolic pressure is called as pulse pressure.

Normal blood pressure of adult male is 120 mm Hg systolic and 80 mmHg diastolic and is expressed as 120/80 mm of Hg.

➢ Procedure

A. Palpatory method

1. Ensure the levels of mercury are at zero mark in sphygmomanometer (figure 14.1) before initiation of the process.
2. Expose the arm up to shoulder, wrap the cuff of sphygmomanometer around the middle arm in such a way that the lowest edge of the cuff remains at a minimum distance of 1 inch above the *cubital fossa*.
3. Palpate the radial artery at the wrist by placing the middle three fingers over it.
4. Hold the rubber bulb in the other hand in such a way that your thumb and index finger remain free to manipulate the leak value screw.
5. Raise the pressure of the mercury manometer by repeatedly compressing the rubber bulb, and continue to feel the radial pulse at the same time. Note the level of mercury in manometer at which pulse disappears this gives systolic pressure,
6. Raise the mercury column up to 10 mmHg above the point of disappearance of the pressure.
7. Reduce the pressure gradually by 2-3 mmHg /sec. Note the mercury level at which the pulse reappears.
8. Decrease the pressure to zero mark.

➢ Advantages

1. Without stethoscope, B.P. can be recorded
2. Is not time consuming.

- ➢ **Disadvantages**
  1. Only suitable for recording of systolic pressure recording.
  2. The systolic pressure is nearly 2-5 mm of Hg less than the actual pressure

B. Ascultatory Method
  1. Follow the same procedures upto step (4).
  2. Raise the pressure 30 mmHg above the palpatory level at which radial pulse disappears.
  3. Place the diaphragm of the stethoscope on the brachial artery (medial side of biceps brachial muscle).
  4. Lower the pressure at a rate of 1-2 mmHg/sec and listen to the appearance of sound and note the level of mercury, this gives systolic B.P.
  5. Slowly, keep on releasing the pressure. The change in sound level (cessation of sound) will give the diastolic B.P. Then note the level of mercury.

- ➢ **Result**

  The blood pressure was found to be .... mmHg by ascultatory method.

- ➢ **Clinical Significance**

  Hypertension : Sustained increase in B.P. than normal level, mainly arterial pressure. A fall in B.P. below normal level is called hypotension.

  Factors responsible for high blood pressure include

  1. **Age :** Blood pressure increases with age.
  2. **Climate :** BP is generally higher in cold atmospheric conditions than in hot condition.
  3. **Exercise :** BP increases with exercise so as to meet the demand of oxygen.
  4. Smokers are more prone to have high BP.
  5. High alcohol consumption may result in high BP
  6. Excess sodium intake with food.
  7. Hormones like adrenaline, noradrenaline, antidiuretic hormone (ADH), angiotensin II, aldosterone etc.
  8. Diabetes, obesity, atherosclerosis/hyperlipidemia are the major disorders due to which BP increases.
  9. **Pheochromocytoma** (tumor of adrenal gland-responsible for continuous release of adrenaline and noradrenaline).

EXERCISE

1. What is blood pressure?
2. How is blood pressure measured? Give the methods of measurement of BP.
3. Give the advantages of palpatory method for BP measurement.
4. Give the normal value of blood pressure and discuss the systolic and diastolic BP.
5. Give the significance of BP measurement.
6. Discuss the various factors responsible for high BP.

EXPERIMENT NO. 15

RECORDING OF PULSE RATE

➢ Aim

To record own pulse rate.

➢ Requirements

Stop watch

➢ Theory

The alternating expansion and recoil of elastic arteries during each cardiac cycle creates a pressure wave called a pulse. Thus, the generation of aortic pressure wave that expands the arterial wall is recorded as pulse. Pulse can be felt at various arteries viz. superficial temporal facial, common carotid, bronchial, femoral, potential, radial etc.

➢ Procedure

1. Palpate the superficial arteries by pressing them against the underlined bones.
2. Usually the radial artery at the wrist position is used for pulse recording.
3. Record the pulse rate for 1 min which is expressed as beats/min.

Result : My own pulse rate was found to be------------ beats/min.

➢ Pathological Significance

Bradycarida : It is a slow resting heart rate; pulse rate is under 60 beats / min.

Tachycardia : Rapid resting heart rate or pulse rate over 100 beats/min is known as tachycardia. Tachycardia can be developed due to release of noradrenalin/adrenaline, exercise, high Na^+ intake etc. Tachycardia may be a contributing factor for hypertension.

Palpitation : Awareness of abnormal heart beat.

EXERCISE

1. Define pulse rate.

2. Give the significance of pulse rate measurement

3. Define the term tachycardia, bradycarida and palpitation

EXPERIMENT NO. 16

RECORDING OF ELECTROCARDIOGRAM

➤ Aim

To record Electrocardiogram (ECG)

➤ Requirements

Electrocardiograph with leads

➤ Theory

Electrical current generated in the heart by action potential can be detected/recorded by ECG on the body surface. This will record the signals generated by heart muscle fibers during each heartbeat. The ECG is recorded by the use of chest leads and limbs leads. These leads positioned on the chest, arms and legs, amplify electrical signals and thus produce various tracings that enable the determination of conduction pathway, size of heart, causes of chest pain and areas of heart damage etc. The instrument used to record these changes is called as an electrocardiograph.

➤ Procedure

1. Ask the subject to lie down and relax.
2. Apply the jelly at left and right wrist and left and right leg above the ankle joint to hold the leads.
3. Connect the electrodes at the above mentioned positions.
4. Switch on the machine and keep the stylus at the centre of the paper.
5. Adjust the sensitive to get standard.
6. Adjust the lead select or knob to record the ECG.
7. Place the chest electors in proper position on the chest after cleaning and application of jelly.
8. Record the ECG and observe various intervals as shown in figure 16.

Following tracing can be observed in normal ECG

P Wave – Deflection produced by atrial depolarisation

QRS complex – Represents rapid ventricular depolarisation. Impaired or abnormal conduction of heart results in widening of QRS complexes

T Wave- Indicates ventricular depolarisation

ST Interval-Represents the time when the ventricular contractile fibers contract during plateau phase. ST intervals increase during myocardial infarction and reduce in coronary ischemia, hypokalemia and digitalis toxicity.

QT Interval - Represents the electrical depolarisation and repolarisation of the left and right ventricles. Prolongation of QT interval is observed in ventricular tachyarrhythmias and shortened QT can be associated with hypercalcemia.

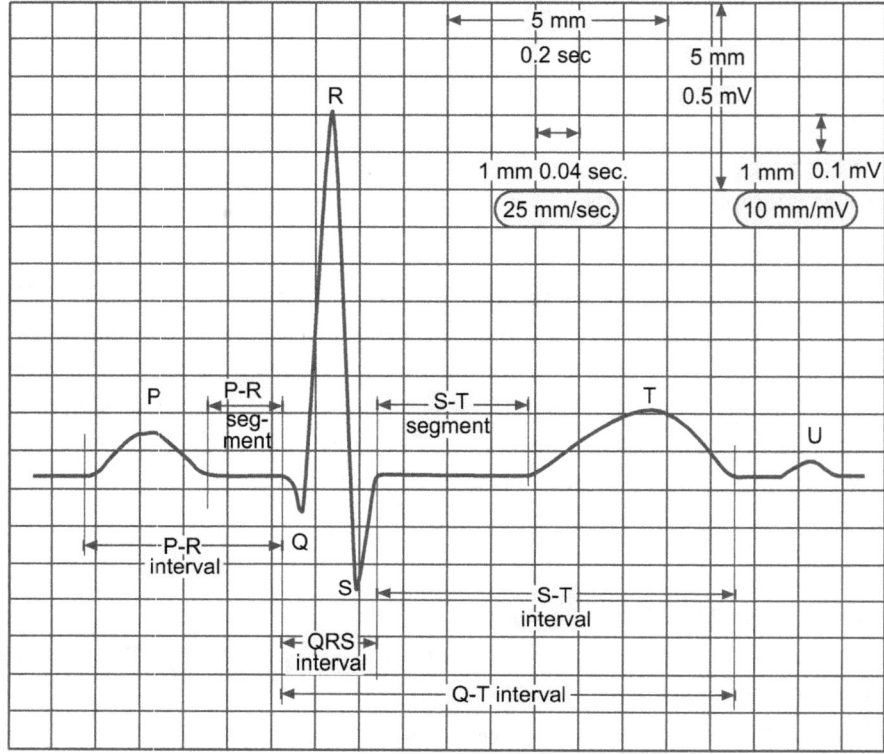

Figure 16.1 : ECG graph

> **Pathological Significance**

1. The use of ECG is used to analyse the relative size of the heart
2. Study of distribution of rhythmical quality and conduction system of heart

Diagnosis of myocardium ischemia, pericarditis caused due to *Mycobacterium* infection and hyperkalemia (high K^+)

EXERCISE

1. What is ECG?
2. Which are the hemodynamic parameters to be recorded by ECG?
3. Give the pathological significance of ECG recording
4. What are ST and QT intervals?
5. What is the significance for Q-T intervals?

❖❖❖

EXPERIMENT NO. 17

MEASUREMENT OF BODY TEMPERATURE

➤ **Aim**

To measure the own body temperature

➤ **Theory**

Body temperature is one of the four main vital signs that must be monitored to ensure safe and effective care; it represents the balance between heat production and heat loss. A healthy body maintains its temperature within a narrow range using homeostatic thermoregulation mechanisms. The normal range for core temperature in the literature varies, although 36°C-37.5°C is acceptable in clinical practice. It is estimated that accompanying every 1°C rise in body temperature is a 10% rise in the rate of enzyme-controlled chemical reactions. The hypothalamus regulates the body temperature through thermostat set in it.

➤ **Techniques of temperature measurement**

1. **Oral cavity-** This route is widely used to measure the body temperature as it is reliable when the thermometer is placed posteriorly into the sublingual pocket.

2. **Tympanic temperature-** The tympanic thermometer senses reflected infrared emissions from the tympanic membrane through a probe placed in the external auditory canal. Advantages of this site are that the measurement is not affected by factors like oral fluids, diet, atmospheric temperature etc.

3. **Axillary temperature-** Temperature is measured at the axilla by placing the thermometer in the central position and adducting the arm close to the chest wall.

4. **Rectal temperature-** Rectal temperature is said to be the most accurate method for measuring the core temperature.

➤ **Procedure**

1. Observe the normal room temperature using clinical thermometer (figure 17.1)

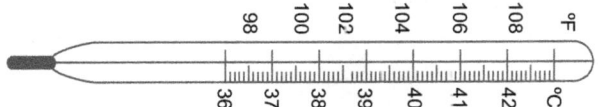

Figure 17.1 : Clinical thermometer

2. Keep the bulb of clinical thermometer in axilla or inside the mouth for a period of 60 seconds,

3. Note the rise of mercury in thermometer as ^0C which indicates the body temperature.

➢ Temperature range and conditions

Hypothermia	<35.0 °C (95.0 °F)
Normal	36.5 – 37.5 °C (97.7 – 99.5 °F)
Fever	>37.5 – 38.3 °C (99.5 – 100.9 °F)
Hyperthermia	>37.5 – 38.3 °C (99.5 – 100.9 °F)
Hyperpyrexia	>40.0 – 41.5 °C (104 – 106.7 °F)

Normal body temperature is **$37^0C \pm 1.0$**.

To convert centigrade into Fahrenheit-multiply ^0C by 9/5, and add 32 (e.g. for 37^0C, 37 × 9/5 = 66.6 + 32 gives 98.6^0F).

To convert Fahrenheit into Centigrade- subtract 32 from ^0F, and multiply by 5/9.

➢ Pathological significance

The body temperature is maintained at a constant level by the thermoregulatory mechanism operated through the hypothalamus in the brain. The change in temperature occurs due to various factors like, exercise, stress, change in atmospheric temperature, cold temperature outside the body etc. An increase in body temperature is known as hyperpyrexia or fever. Fever is body's defense mechanism, and is considered to be the main and important sign of bacterial infection.

EXERCISE

1. What is fever?
2. Enlist different methods for measurement of body temperature.
3. Give the significance of temperature measurement.
4. What is pyrexia? Give its importance.

EXPERIMENT NO. 18

DETERMINATION AND RECORDING OF RESPIRATORY VOLUME

➢ Aim

To determine and record the respiratory volumes in human subject

➢ Theory

Respiratory volumes are the volumes of air which are exchanged during breathing, and indicate proper functioning of the respiratcry system. Respiratory volumes are measured with the help of a device called as spirometer. The spirometer consists of outer and inner jackets and a bell. The outer jacket is filled with water (quantity) and is opened from upper side, while inner jacket is a closed one (figure 18.1).

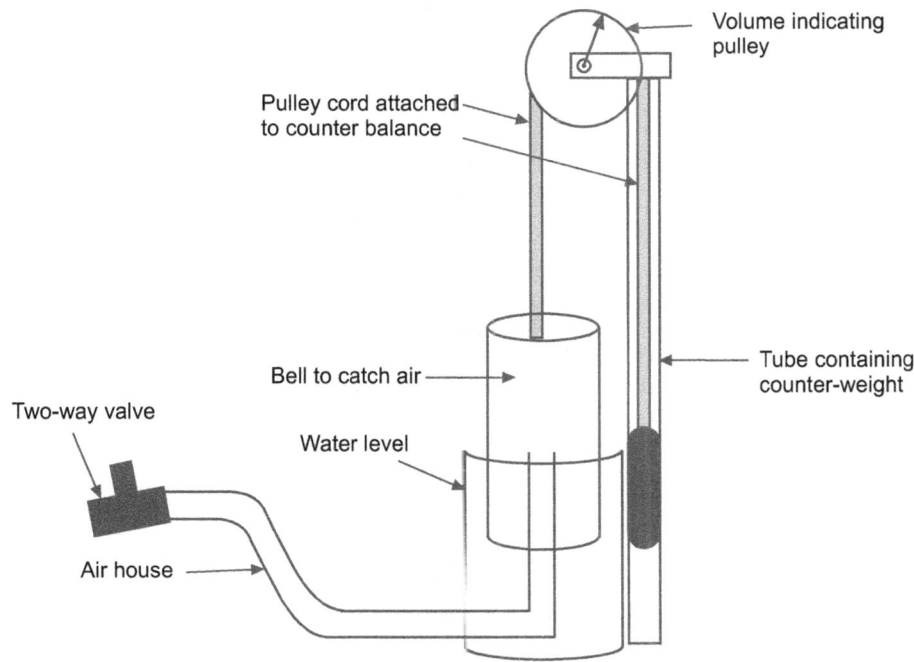

Figure 18.1 : Spirometer

The metal tube pierces (penetrate) the bottom of the spirometer and elevates over the inner jacket and is attached to a rubber tube having mouth piece from another end. The individual is asked to breathe through this mouth piece. The outer jacket holds the spirometer bell (smaller metallic cylinder) that is completely immersed in the water and is balanced by weight.

➢ Principle

The spirometer bell is suspended through a beaded chain which is run over a pulley to a writing lever to record the level of the bell on a slow rotating drum.

➢ Procedure

1. Assemble the spirometer properly to working position and adjust the pointer in the middle of the drum which moves constantly at a slow speed.

2. Hold the rubber mouth piece in the mouth. The clip is applied to nose so that inspiration and expiration must be take place through mouth only. The normal inspiration and expiration through mouth gives tidal volume. *Tidal volume* is the volume of air taken in or given out during normal breathing (normal tidal volume is 500 ml).

3. Breathe normally, and inspire forcefully, this gives inspiratory reserve volume (IRV). The inspiratory reserve volume is the volume of air that can be taken in by forced inspiration over and above normal breathing (normal IRV is 2000-3300 ml).

4. Record the normal respiration, and again expire forcefully; resulting air volume is termed as expiratory reserve volume. The expiratory reserve volume is the volume of air that can be breathed out by forced expiration after normal expiration (normal expiratory reserve volume is 1000 ml).

5. Inspire maximally and expire completely into the spirometer, this gives the vital capacity. The vital capacity is the sum of inspiratory reserve volume, tidal volume

and expiratory reserve volume i.e. the volume of air that can be taken in by forced expiration after forced inspiration (normal vital capacity is 4800 ml in males and 3100 in females).

6. Breathe normal, and inspire deeply and forcefully for 15 sec. The air that remains in the lungs is the total lung capacity. Therefore, the total lung capacity is the sum of vital capacity and residual volume i.e. the volume of air remaining in the lungs after deep and forceful inspiration (normal total lung capacity is 4800 + 1200 = 6000 ml)

7. Take normal breath and expire maximally; whatever air remains in the lungs is the residual volume. Therefore, the residual volume is the volume of air which remains in the lungs after maximum expiration (normal residual volume is 1200 ml).

Normal values of respiratory capacity are

Tidal volume -	500 ml
Inspiratory reserve volume-	2000-3000 ml
Expiratory reserve volume-	1000 ml
Vital capacity-	4800 ml in males, 3100 ml in females
Total lung capacity	6000 ml
Residual volume	1200 ml

Minute ventilation-is the normal tidal volume multiplied by inhalation and exhalation per minute (normally, healthy adults averages 12 breaths/minute)

Hence, Minute ventilation =12 breaths/min × 500 = 6000 ml/minute

> ## Pathological significance

Vital capacity is impaired in diseased conditions viz. pulmonary tuberculosis, pneumonia, emphysema, pulmonary congestion etc.

EXERCISE

1. Give the uses of spirometer.
2. Explain the working of spirometer.
3. Give the pathological significance of respiratory volumes.
4. Define the following terminologies with their normal values
   (a) Tidal volume
   (b) Inspiratory reserve volume
   (c) Expiratory reserve volume
   (d) Vital capacity
   (e) Total lung capacity
   (f) Residual volume

❖ ❖ ❖

EXPERIMENT NO. 19

DETERMINATION OF BREATH HOLDING TIME AND HYPERVENTILATION TIME

➢ Aim

To determine the breath holding time (BHT), hyperventilation time in humans

➢ Requirements

Stethograph, Kymograph, Marey's tambour.

Stethograph is an instrument used for determining the movements of changes in the air pressure of chest (figure 19.1), these changes are recorded on kymograph (figure 19.3)

Marey's tambour - it is made up of metallic cup with tube and rubber diaphragm mounted on the top. The writing lever is joined to a metal disc which lies on the diaphragm (figure 19.2)

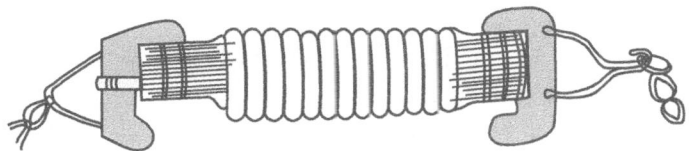

Figure 19.1: Stethograph

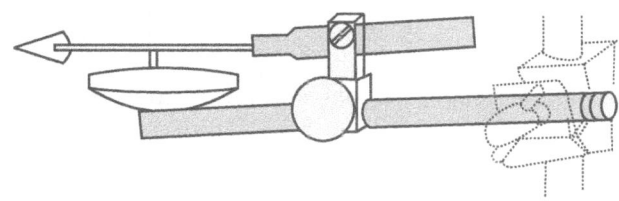

Figure 19.2: Marey's tambour

➢ Procedure

1. Ask the individual to sit on a chair or stool opposite to the rotating drum with kymograph.
2. Tie the stethograph to the chest of the individual exactly at fourth intercostals space (figure 19.4) and start the rotating drum (whole assembly consists of kymograph, writing lever touching the pointer on kymograph at a speed of 1.25-2.5).

3. Record the normal respiration for 5 minutes (as shown in figure 19.3).
4. Ask the individual to hold the breath for quite some time, and again hold the breath after inspiration as long as possible and record the time. The person then should be asked to breathe normally, hold the breath after expiration as long as possible and record the same.

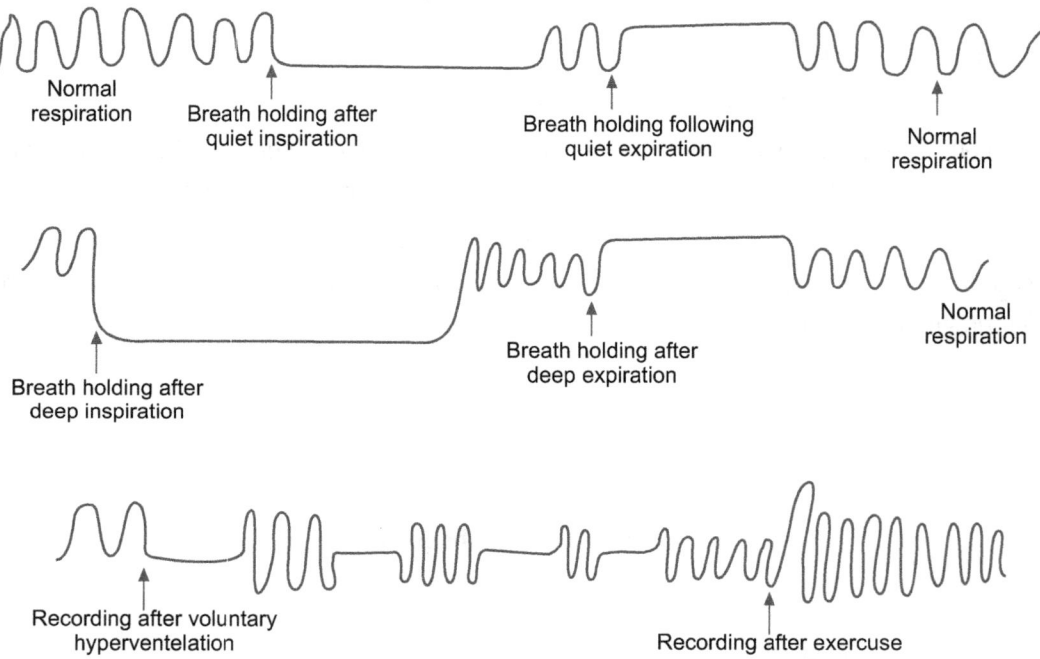

Figure 19.3 : Recording of various respiratory changes on kymograph

5. Ask the individual to hyperventilate for up to 2 minutes and record the breathing time.
6. Ask the individual to respire normally, remove the stethograph from the chest, and then ask the individual to exercise (running, other activity). Immediately after the exercise, place the stethograph on the chest and connect it to tambour and record the changes of respiratory movement.

Normal breath holding time : 30-50 sec.

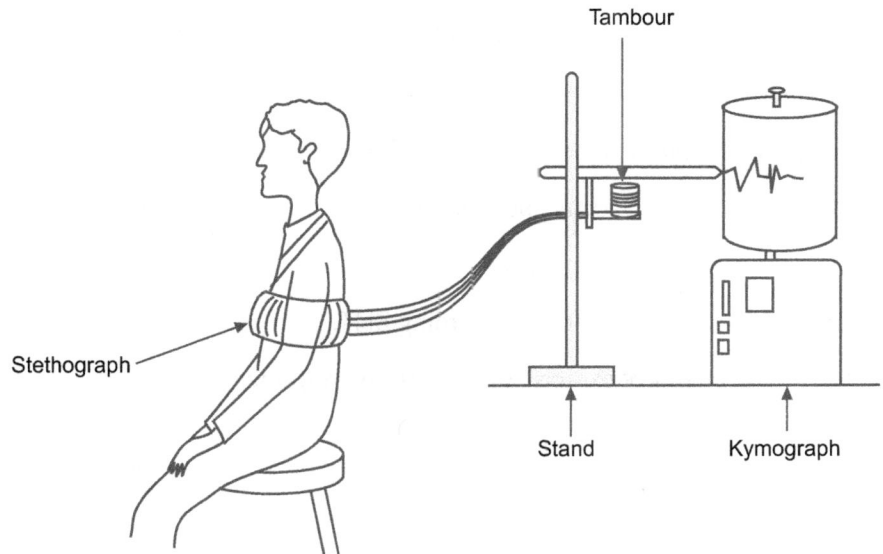

Figure 19.4: Setup of stethograph and recording of breath holding and hyperventilation time

Cheyne-stroke respiration-It is characterised by alternative apnea (difficulty in breathing) and hyperventilation. It is predominantly observed in left ventricular failure and brain damage.

Exercise also affects breathing due to activation of respiratory centre by hyperactivity of ligaments and skeletal muscles. It results in increased oxygen utilisation by tissues.

➢ Clinical significance

Breath holding time (BHT) - it is the time taken by an individual to hold his/her breath as long as possible. The BHT is found to be higher after inspiration compared to expiration. The breaking point suggests that the breathing cannot be held back voluntarily by an individual because of increase in carbon dioxide, reduction of oxygen in blood plasma, and uneven oxygen utilisation by the tissues.

In asthma, BHT is reduced and it may range from 5 to 15 sec depending upon the severity of asthma. Inhalation of 100 % pure oxygen increases BHT due to delay in breaking point. Hyperventilation also increases BHT due to quick removal of carbon dioxide from blood and thus delays in breaking point.

EXERCISE

1. Give the functions of stethograph.
2. What is breath holding time (BHT)? Give the normal BHT.
3. Enlist and discuss the factors affecting BHT.
4. What is Cheyne-stroke respiration?
5. Give the clinical significance of recording BHT.
6. What are the effects of exercise on respiratory movements?

❖ ❖ ❖

EXPERIMENT NO. 20

DETERMINATION OF VISUAL ACUITY FOR NEAR AND DISTANCE VISION

➤ **Aim**

To determine the visual acuity for near and distant vision of subject

➤ **Requirements**

Jaeger's chart and Snellen chart

Test for Near Point Vision

➤ **Principle**

The visual acuity is the resolving power of the eyes. The rods and cones are the important components of eyes in the visual acuity. Visual acuity for near point is performed by the use of Jaeger's chart at a distance of normal reading. The Jaeger's chart is prepared as per the principle of printer's point system (employs prints of different sizes which are read at a distance of 30 cm from the eyes under standard illumination).

N_5
The central nervous system consists of the brain and spinal cord. The brain is an important organ of nervous system and spinal cord is involved in various functions. mainly transmission of sensory information from parts of body to the highest centre. The spinal cord is the origin for the various nerves i.e. nerves form spinal cord supplies to various organs.
N_6
Visual acuity for near point is performed by the use of Jaeger's chart from the distance of normal reading. The Jaeger's chart is prepared as per the principle of printer's point system (employs prints of different sizes which are read at a distance of 30 cm under standard illumination).
N_8
Breath holding time is the time taken by an individual to hold his/her breath as long as possible. The breaking point suggests that breathing cannot be held back voluntarily by an individual because of increase in carbon dioxide, reduction of oxygen in blood plasma, and uneven oxygen utilisation by the tissues.
N_{10}
The human chorionic gonadotrophic hormone secreted after 6 days of fertilisation, it is necessary for the maintenance of corpus luteum at the beginning of pregnancy and secrete progesterone.

Figure 20.1 : Jaeger's chart

N5-N6 is the near normal acuity. The Jaeger's chart has letters ranging in size from N5- the smallest to N36- the largest (as shown in figure 20.1)

➤ Procedure

1. Keep the room under normal illumination (well lit) and ask the subject to sit on a chair or stool and relax.
2. Place the Jaeger's chart at a distance of 30 cm from the individual.
3. Ask him to read the letters on Jaeger's chart.
4. Perform the procedure individually for both eyes (one eye closed and the other eye open).
5. Note the number which can be easily and comfortably read from the 30 cm distance

Test for Distant Vision

➤ Principle

To test for distant vision, the Snellen chart (figure 20.2) is employed. It consists of various alphabetical letters of different sizes. Letter are of the sizes 60, 36, 24, 18 which means that the top letter is clearly visible to normal eyes from 60 meters and subsequent lines of letters from 36, 24, 18 and 9 meters respectively. Visual acuity is determined by the formula

$$\text{Visual acuity} = \frac{\text{Distance at which the letter is read (6 meters)}}{\text{Distance at which the letter should be read}}$$

➤ Procedure

1. The room in which test is performed should be well illuminated.
2. Ask the individual to read the letter of Snellen's chart with one eye closed
3. Note the line that should be read easily by the individual
4. Repeat the same procedure with the other eye.

➤ Observation

The visual acuity is 6/60 if the letters are visible (6-distance from which the letter is read and 60-for the top letter). If the individual can read the letter of the lowest line then visual acuity is 6/5 indicating good vision. The normal visual acuity is 6/6.

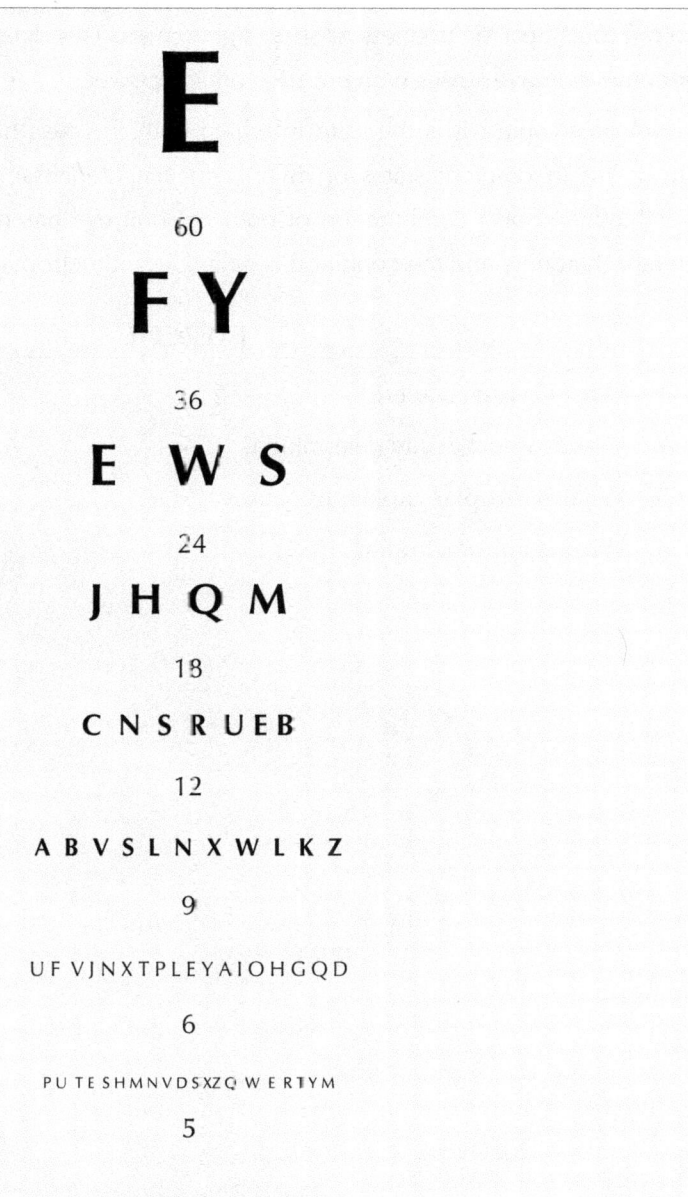

Figure 20.2 : Snellen's chart

- ### Clinical significance

Myopia : It is characterised by the inability to see distant objects. It occurs when light rays coming from outside directly focus in front of the retina. As a result, the image of the retina is formed in front of the retina instead of forming on the retina. This condition is also referred to as near sightedness or short sightedness. This defect can be corrected by use of corrective concave lenses with negative optical power.

Anisometropia : It is the state in which both the eyes have uneven refractive power, that is, are in different states of myopia (nearsightedness), hyperopia or hypermetropia (farsightedness) or a combination of both i.e. one eye has nearsightedness and the other one farsightedness and the condition is called as antimetropia

EXERCISE

1. What is visual acuity?
2. How is visual acuity determined?
3. What is myopia? Explain its causes
4. What is anisometropia?

EXPERIMENT NO. 21

DETERMINATION OF DOMINANCE OF EYE

➢ Aim

To determine the dominance of one's own eye.

➢ Requirements

A piece of paper

➢ Principle

It is the tendency to prefer visual input from one eye to the other eye.

Procedure

Dominance of eye can be determined by Dolman method in laboratory

1. Take a piece of paper, and give a cut to its centre to make a small hole of 1 inch diameter.
2. Hold the paper with both the hands at the arm's length in front of you.
3. Look at any near non movable object (chair, any point etc) through the hole on paper.
4. Continue the focus and gradually bring the paper closer to the eyes until it touches your face.
5. You will find the hole is front of one of eye i.e. the dominant eye.

Clinical significance : In most people, right eye is dominant over the left eye. Dominance appears due to changes as per the direction toward object; this is due to change in image size on retina.

EXERCISE

1. What is dominance of eye?
2. Give the principle involved in determination of dominance of the eye.
3. Give the clinical significance of dominance of the eye.

EXPERIMENT NO. 22

DETERMINATION OF SPECIAL SENSES

➢ Aim

To determine special senses (smell and taste)

Determination of Smell

➢ Requirements

Bottles with clove oil and peppermint oil

➢ Principle

Sensation of smell is called as olfaction. This function is mediated by olfactory receptors on the olfactory bulb and its activation is caused due to odorant molecules. The olfaction is higher in animals comparatively to human beings.

➢ Procedure

1. Ask the individual to sit on a chair or stool and clean the nose (it should not contain mucus as it observed during allergic rhinitis or inflammation of nose).
2. Ask him/her to close both eyes and one of the nostrils.
3. Open the cap of the bottle containing peppermint oil and keep it near the open nostril.
4. Ask him/her to smell the bottle and note the smell.
5. Repeat the same procedure for clove oil.
6. Repeat steps 1 to 5 for the other nostril.
7. Compare the smell from both the nostrils.
8. Note the results as per the following degree of smell from both the nostrils by tick mark

Characteristic of smell	First nostril	Second nostril
Normal smell		
Reduced smell		
No smell		

➤ **Clinical significance**

Anosmia : It is characterised by the inability of a person to smell, it might occur due to tumour of olfactory bulb, common cold and or allergic rhinitis.

Dysosmia : Dysosmia, also known as **olfactory dysfunction**, is the impairment of olfactory stimuli processing leading to an altered sense of smell.

Olfactory reference syndrome : It is a psychological disorder in which the patient imagines that he/she has a strong unpleasant body odour.

Determination of Taste

➤ **Requirements**

Four dishes containing strong solutions of sweet (sugar), salt (common salt), sour (lime juice) and bitter solution of quinine. Glassware should also include a clean glass stirrer.

➤ **Principle**

Facial (VII), glossopharyngeal (IX) and vagus (X) nerves are involved in perceiving the sense of taste from the particular receptors located on the various regions of the tongue.

➤ **Procedure**

1. Ask the individual to close his/her eyes and extend his/her tongue
2. Dip the stirrer into the sweet solution and place on various parts of tongue, and ask him/her to tell the taste of solution and note the taste.
3. Rinse the mouth with fresh water and repeat the same procedure for the salt, sour and finally for the bitter solution (mouth should be rinsed before testing of every solution).

➤ **Clinical significance**

The taste receptors are located in the taste buds which are found on the papillae of the tongue. The four basic tastes are sweet, bitter, salt and sour at different regions of the tongue.

Sweet-receptors are located on the tip of tongue; bitter-receptors are located at the back of the tongue, salt-receptors are located at the centre of dorsum of the tongue; and sour-receptors are located on the lateral sides of the tongue.

The impaired taste is an absence of taste (metallic taste) caused due to various factors mainly common cold, normal ageing, drug treatments (metronidazole, tinidazole etc) or sinus infection.

Gingivitis : It is the inflammation of the gum. Head or ear injuries and vitamin B_{12} deficiency also results in impaired taste.

EXERCISE

1. Give the principle of sense of smell
2. What are olfactory receptors? Explain their role in perceiving smell?
3. What is anosmia, dysosmia and olfactory reference syndrome?
4. Give the principle of sense of taste.
5. Enlist the various tastes with their regions of perception on the tongue.
6. What is the clinical significance of sense of taste?

EXPERIMENT NO. 23

STUDY OF HUMAN CELLS, TISSUES AND HISTOLOGY OF ORGANS

➢ Aim

To study human cells, tissue and histology of various organs.

➢ Theory

Cell is the basic structural, functional and biological unit of all known living microorganisms. Cells are also known as building blocks of life. Cells when grouped together, form tissue. Number of different tissues together form an organ and finally a number of organs form the body's systems. The cell is made up of plasma membrane, organelles, cytoplasm, nucleus, mitochondria, ribosome, endoplasmic reticulum, Golgi apparatus, lysosomes and the cytoskeleton (figure 23.1).

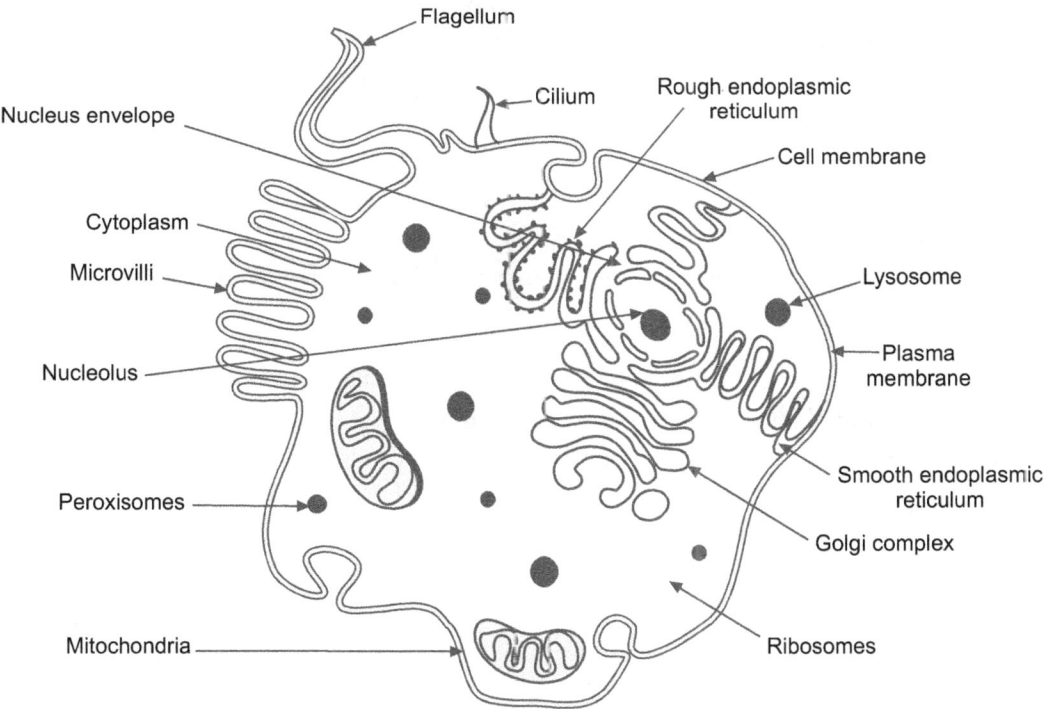

Figure 23.1 : Human Cell

The plasma membrane consists of phospholipids and proteins and acts as a barrier against flow of materials inside and outside the cell. The cytoplasm consists of cellular contents within the plasma membrane and nucleus. Organelles have characteristic shape and specific function in cellular growth, maintenance and reproduction. Nucleus contains the genetic material deoxyribonucleic acid (DNA) which controls the various metabolic functions of the body. Nucleus also has aggregates of loosely packed granules consisting of ribonucleic acid (RNA), it matures during protein synthesis which aid to regulate the cytoplasmic functions. Mitochondria is known as the powerhouse of the cell as they serve as store house of energy in the form of ATP (adenine triphosphate).Mitochondria are essential in cells involved in aerobic respiration. The ribosomes are composed of RNA and amino acids, and line the endoplasmic reticulum. The endoplasmic reticulum is the interconnection of canals in the cytoplasm and is involved in the synthesis of steroidal hormones, lipids, proteins and in the detoxification of drugs. Golgi apparatus consists of a continuous series of flat membranous sacs and appears as vesicles which secrete the proteins outside the cell by exocytosis. The lysosomes are filled with a large number of granules which are aggregates of digestive enzymes which aid in the digestion of cell components (proteins, nucleic acid and glycogen). Cytoskeleton is made up of an extensive network of tiny protein fibers, microfilaments which offer support and maintain the particular shape of the cell. The microtubules are the contractile protein fibers responsible for the movement of organelles inside the cell, chromosome and cell extension. The cilia are hair like projections with micotubules responsible for movement of substance along the cell surface; similarly, microvilli are tiny projections on the cell surface, which help in absorption of nutrients. The flagella are whip like projections that forms the tail of the sperm, enabling their movement along the female reproductive tract.

> **Tissue**

Tissue is a group of cells and involved in various activities and functions of the body. Tissues are classified into various types as per their arrangement and location in body.

There are main four types of tissues

1. Epithelial tissue
2. Connective tissue
3. Muscular tissue
4. Nervous tissue

1. Epithelial tissue-It lies on the body surface, lines the hollow organs, body cavities and ducts, forms glands and it interacts with external and internal environment during activity of the organ. The different types of epithelial tissue are given in the table below.

Simple squamous epithelium : It is single layer flat cells. The cells have oval or spherical nucleus and constitute the layers of heart, blood vessels, lymphatic vessels, peritoneum, lungs, and kidneys. This tissue helps in the process of filtration and diffusion.	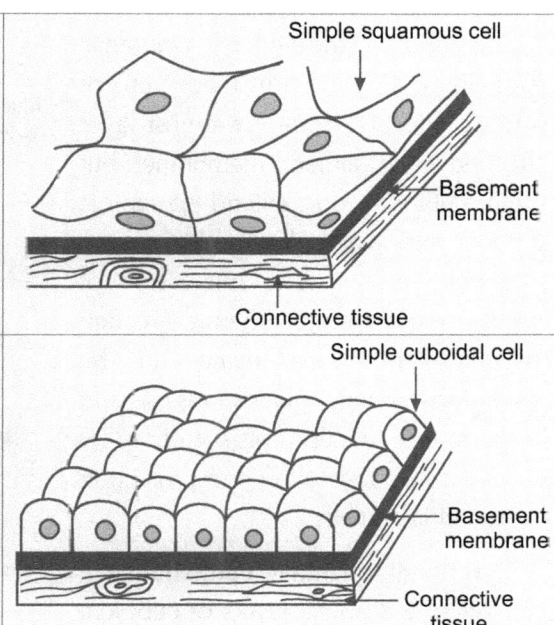
Simple cuboidal epithelium : This tissue is round, cube shaped, provides covering to the ovary, eyes, and smaller secretory ducts like thyroid and pancreas and helps in secretion and absorption.	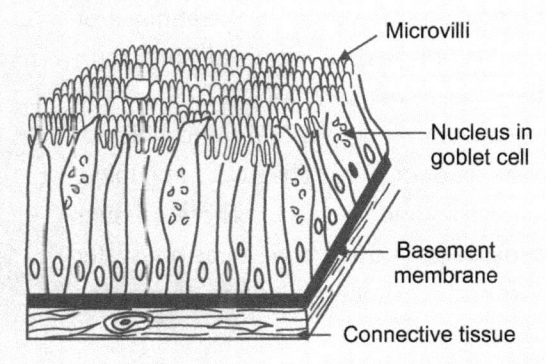
Nonciliated columnar epithelium : It is composed of non nucleated column like cells having fingerlike projections called microvilli which increase the surface area resulting in faster absorption. A type of cell of this tissue is the globet cell which secretes sticky fluid called the mucus which aids in the lubrication of female reproductive tract and respiratory tract.	
Ciliated simple columnar epithelium : The ciliated columnar cells form goblet cells are found on inner side of the bronchioles, fallopian tubes, uterus, nose, and brain. These tissue helps in movement of particles/mucus towards mouth, ovum towards uterus through fallopian tubes	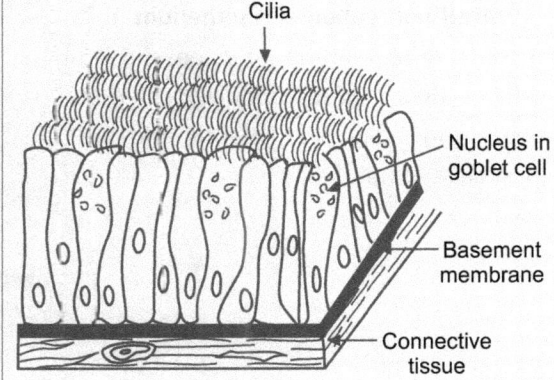

Pseudo stratified columnar epithelium : They are made up of various layers with the lowermost layer attached to basement membrane, but some cells do not extend to apical surface, and when observed from the side, they give a false impression of being multilayered; hence called 'pseudo'. These are located in the respiratory system, glands, testes, and perform the function of secretion by ciliated cells; absorption and protection by non ciliated cells

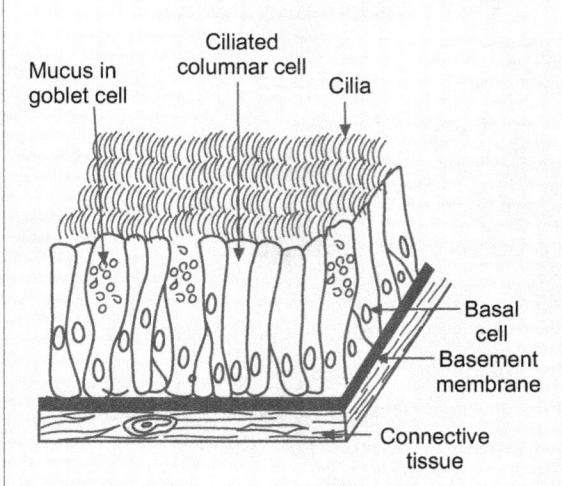

Stratified squamous epithelium : It consists of 2-3 apical layers of cuboidal or columnar cells. The cells are hard and tough. They may be keratinised or non keratinised. Keratinised cells form the uppermost layer of the skin, while non keratinised cells line the cavities of the mouth, esophagus, epiglottis, pharynx and vagina. These tissues provide protection from abrasion, water loss and prevent entry of foreign matter.

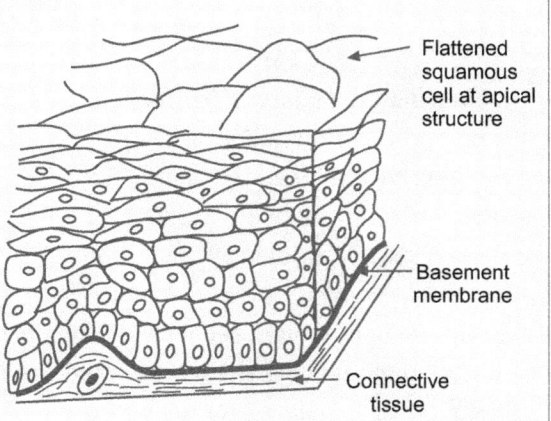

Stratified cuboidal epithelium : It consists of 2-3 layers of cube shaped cells of the apical membrane located in sweat and esophageal glands and are protective in function.

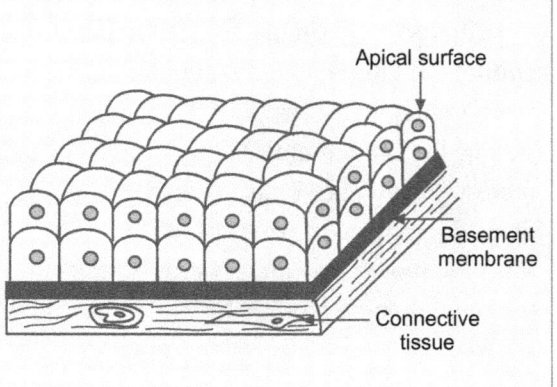

Stratified columnar epithelium : It consists of short, irregular columnar cells found lining the urethra and glands. These tissues help in protection and secretion.

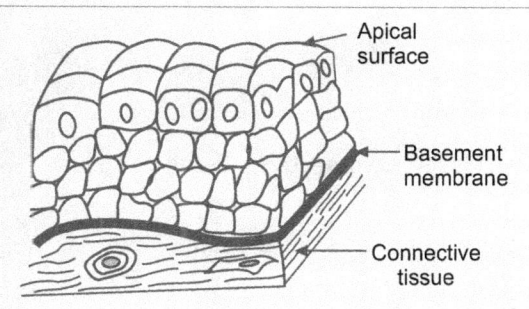

Transitional epithelium : Named so because of their variable shapes at different states i.e. they appears as cuboidal epithelium in relaxed state, flat and squamous in contracted state. Found in the urinary and reproductive tracts and help during contraction and relaxation of the organs of these systems

2. **Connective tissue-** This is the most widespread and abundant type of biological tissue of the human body and serves a "connecting" function along with protection, support to organs and providing immunity against various infectious diseases.

Areolar connective tissue : It is made up of collagen, reticular and elastic fibers adjacent to fibroblasts.

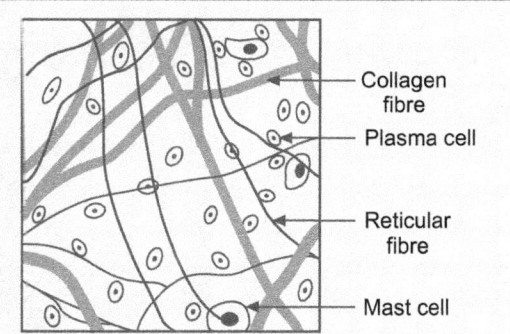

Adipose tissue : Each cell of this tissue consists of a single, large droplet of triglycerides. This tissue lies in subcutaneous layer of skin, heart, kidney and eye and serves as energy reserve. Also helps to support and protect the organs.

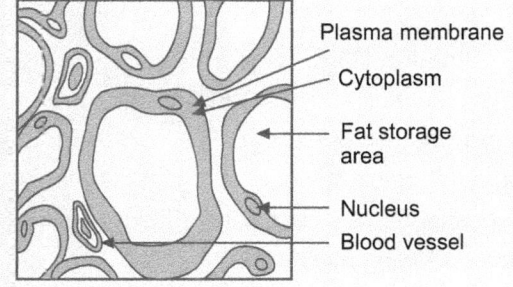

Human Anatomy and Physiology　　　　81　　　　An Experimental Handbook

Reticular connective tissue : These are fine interlacing network of reticular fibers and cells, located in liver, spleen, lymph node, blood vessels etc.	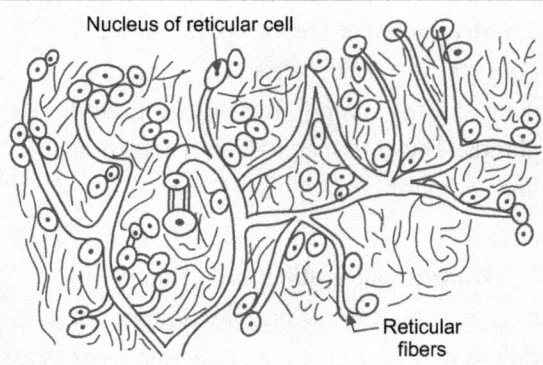
Elastic connective tissue : This tissue is elastic in nature and found inside fibroblasts. Also found in lungs, arteries, trachea, and suspensory ligaments. Functions during the stretching of organs.	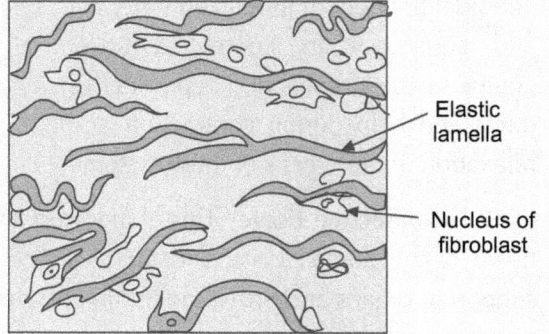
Bone : Consists of osteons having osteocyts, canaculi, lacunae. It offers support, protection, storage; and acts as blood forming tissue.	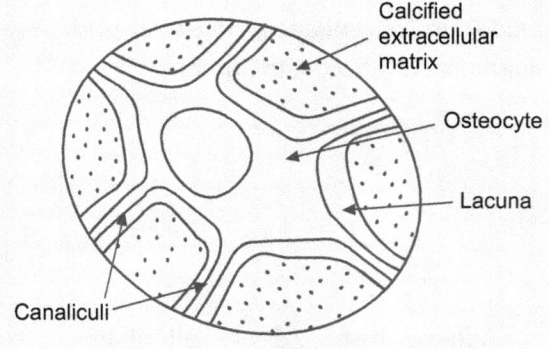
Blood : Consists of RBCs, WBCs, and platelets. The RBCs help in transportation of CO_2 and O_2, WBCs in immunological functions, phagocytosis and allergic reactions; and platelets in blood clotting mechanism	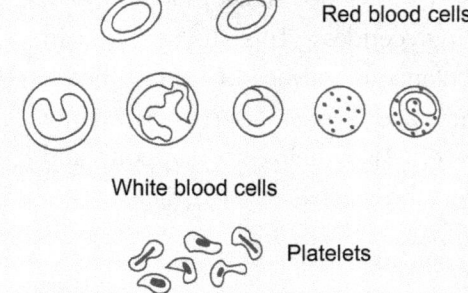

3. Muscular tissue : It is composed of elongated muscle cells, categorized as either striated or smooth muscle cells depending on the presence or absence, respectively, of organised, regularly repeated arrangements of myofilaments that helps in contraction and relaxation during body movement, maintenance of posture and heat generation.

Skeletal muscle : It is long, striated and has 20-40 cm long cylindrical fibers and are attached to the bone with the help of tendons, functions during body movement and heat production. Skeletal muscles are voluntary in nature, work under conscious control.	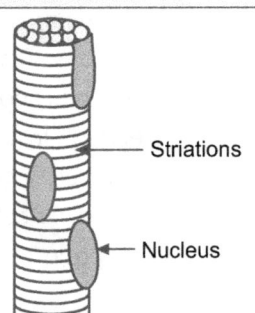
Cardiac muscle : It is branched, striated with intercalated disc, found in heart. Helps in contraction and relaxation of the heart and thus pumps the blood to the body organs. It is involuntary in nature.	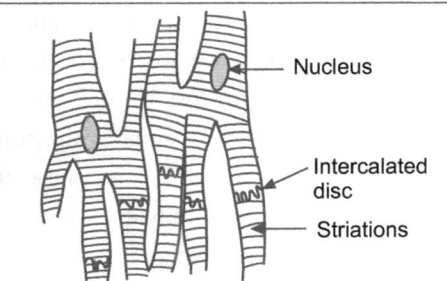
Smooth muscle : It is non-striated, small, spindle shaped, having single nucleus at the centre .It is found in the iris of the eye, visceral organs (blood vessels, lungs, stomach, intestine, urinary bladder, uterus, and stomach). It is involuntary in nature.	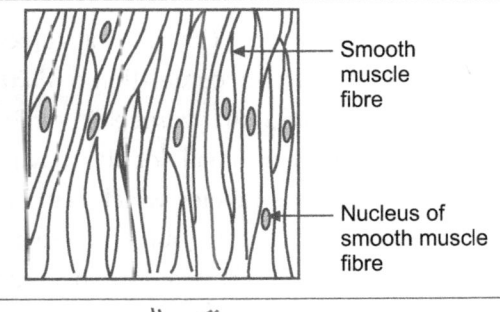
Nervous tissue : Nervous tissue is made up of neurons which consist of cell body with dendrites, axons. They form the nervous system. The nerve cell senses the particular stimuli and converts it into the action potential, which is conducted to glands, neurons and muscle etc.	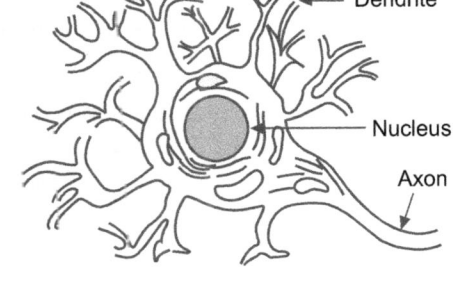

Histology of various organs

T.S. of pancreas : 99 % of the exocrine cells of the pancreas called as acini, are arranged in clusters. They produce pancreatic enzymes; remaining 1 % of the cells forms the islet cells. These secrete hormones such as α- glucagon (increase glucose), β-cells secrete insulin (reduce glucose), δ cells secrete stomatostatin (regulate growth) and f-cells secrete pancreatic polypeptide (decrease somatostatin).

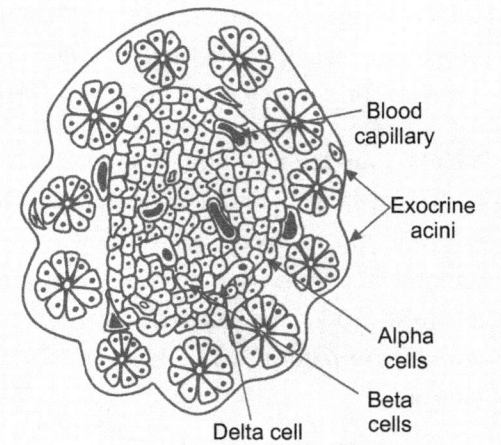

T. S. of liver : Hepatocytes are the important cells involved in metabolic and secretary activity, form the 80-85 % of total liver cells and contain hepatic sinusoids. The hepatic laminae are the plate like arrangement of hepatocytes and are responsible for bile secretion.

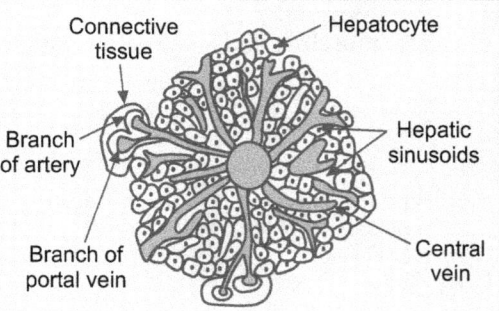

T. S. of Testis : Consists of tunica vaginalis (outer layer-accumulation of fluids in this layer results in hydrocele), tunica albuginia consists of small lobules having several somniferous tubules which serve in sperm production. Within tubules, there are spermatogonic cells (sperm forming) and sertoli cells (helping in sperm production). The Leydig cells are found in between somniferous tubes and secrete testosterone (sex hormone) and might be responsible for sexual arousal in men

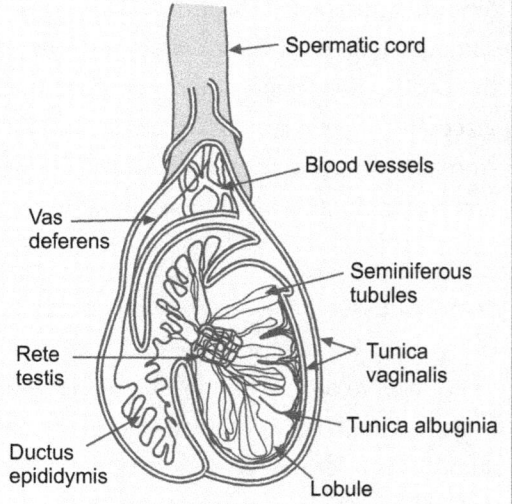

Human Anatomy and Physiology   **An Experimental Handbook**

T. S. of ovary : Each ovary is compact with cortex and medulla. The cortex contains follicles and corpora lutea in various forms. It is made up of reticular fibrous tissues. The female gametes, eggs/ova in various stages remain enclosed in the form of scattered ovarian follicles. Out of several primordial follicles, only one get matures into graafian follicle each month.

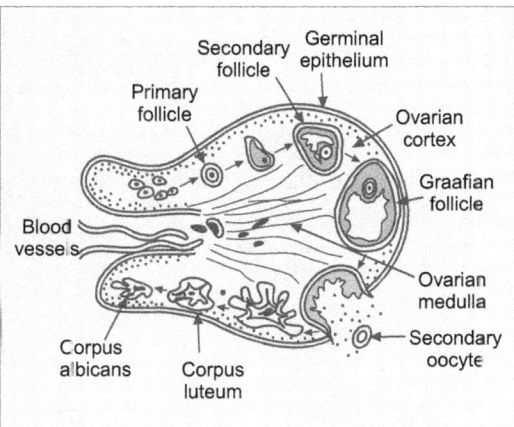

T. S. of adrenal gland : It is made up of zona glomerulosa, an outer layer having closely packed cells which secrete mineralocorticoids. Zona fasiculata is the middle zone, between the glomerulosa and reticularis consisting of cells which secrete glucocorticoids .The innermost layer zona reticularis secrete androgen. The adrenal medulla contains chromaffin cells which secrete adrenaline.

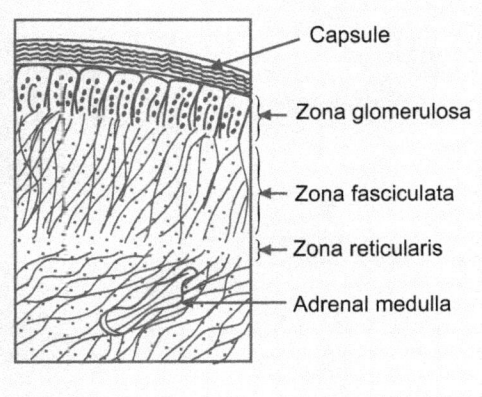

T. S. of thyroid gland : It consists of spherical sacs known as thyroid follicles made up of surrounding follicular cells and parafollicular cells in between. Thyroid follicles secrete thyroxine and triiodothyronine (thyroid hormones), while parafollicular cells secrete calcitonin (regulate calcium homeostasis).

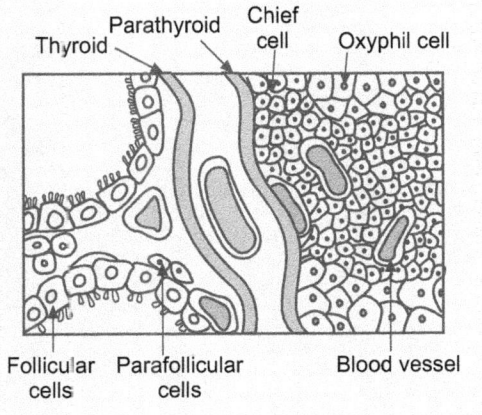

EXERCISE

1. Define the cell and enlist various components of cell
2. What is tissue? Give the difference between cell and tissue
3. Give the classification of tissue with examples
4. Give the locations of epithelial, connective, muscular and nervous tissues in human body.

EXPERIMENT NO. 24

STUDY OF THE CARDIOVASCULAR SYSTEM

➢ **Aim**

To study the cardiovascular system

➢ **Theory**

Cardiovascular (Cardio- cardiac heart, vascular- blood vessels) system consists of heart, blood and blood vessels (arteries, arterioles, veins, venules and capillaries).

Blood is a connective tissue composed of a liquid extracellular matrix called blood plasma that contains dissolved substances and contains various cells and cells fragments suspended in it. Blood transports oxygen and nutrients.

Blood flows from heart towards blood vessels or from blood vessels to heart. This function is carried out by its pumping action and therefore heart acts as a pump.

1. HEART

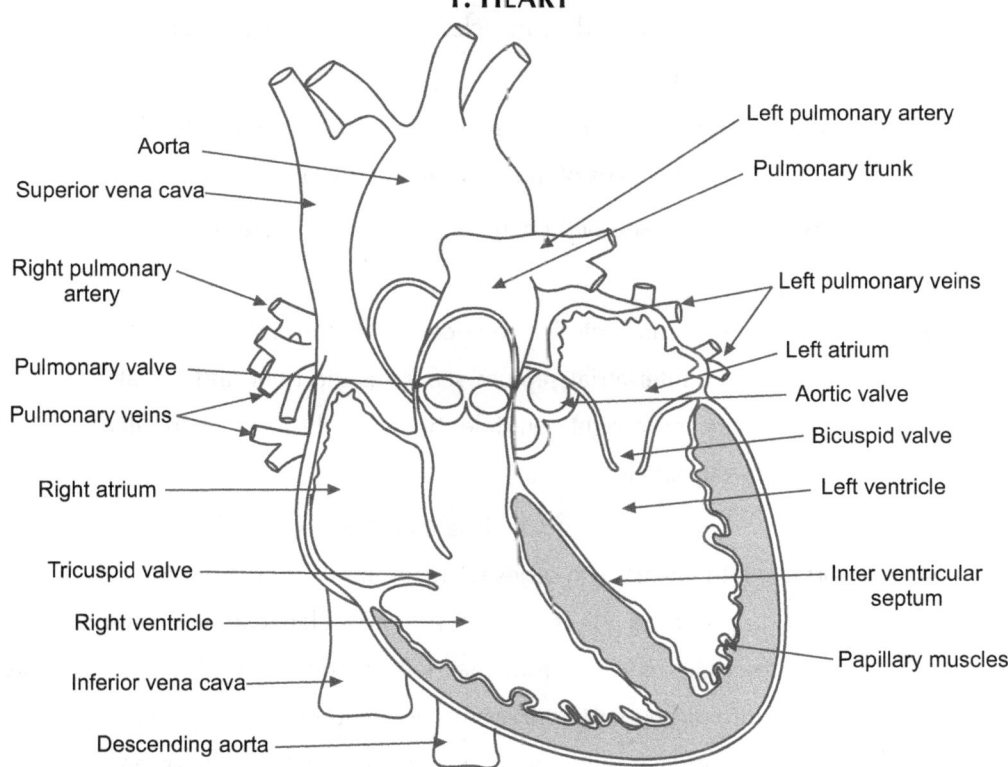

Figure 24.1 : The Human Heart

Anatomy of the heart

(A) Location of the heart : The heart lies between vertebral column and lungs. 1/3rd of the heart is located slightly toward the left of the body's midline, resting on the diaphragm adjacent to thoracic cavity. Right border faces the right lung and extends from interior surface to the base. Left border faces the left lung and extends from the base to the apex.

(B) Size and shape of heart : It is 12 cm long, 9 cm wide 6 cm thick with about 250-300 gm weight in adult.

(C) Layers of heart

(a) **Pericardium :** It is the membrane that surrounds and protects the heart.

(b) **Epicardium :** It is the inner visceral layer of the pericardium. It imparts a smooth and slippery texture to the outer surface of the heart.

(c) **Myocardium :** Involuntary cardiac muscle, its contraction and relaxation property responsible for pumping action.

(d) **Endocardium :** Innermost layer of heart which imparts smooth lining to the heart chamber and covers the valves of the heart (figure 24.1).

(D) Heart chambers : It is composed of 4 chambers, two atria superiorly and two ventricles inferiorly.

(a) **Right atrium :** Superior and inferior vena cava and coronary sinus drain the blood into the right atrium. Inter-atrial septum separates the right and left atrium. Blood moves from right atrium to right ventricle through right atrio-ventricular (A.V.) and tricuspid (3 points cups) valves.

(b) **Right ventricle :** The right ventricle is about 4-5 mm thick, forming the most anterior surface of the heart. The series of ridges are the manifestation due to raised bundle of cardiac muscle fibers known as trabeculae carneae. Interventricular septum separates right ventricle from the left ventricle. Blood moves into larger artery and then into pulmonary trunk from right ventricle through pulmonary valve, which divides right and left pulmonary arteries and carries blood towards lungs.

(c) Left atrium : Left atrium is almost identical to that of right atrium, receives blood through 4 pulmonary veins. Bicuspid valve (mitral) is also called as left AV valve through which oxygenated blood moves from left atrium to left ventricle.

(d) Left ventricle : It is similar to the right ventricle. The left ventricle contains trabeculae carneae and chordate tendinae that connect the cups of mitral value to papillary muscle. Blood from left ventricle passes toward ascending aorta through aortic valve. Some quantity of blood also flows into the coronary artery, which branch from the ascending aorta and carry blood to the heart wall. Oxygenated blood for all the parts of body is supplied from arch of the aorta and descending aorta.

All valves (right and left AV valve, aortic and pulmonary valve) help to ensure the one way flow of blood by opening to maintain the flow of blood through them and then closing to prevent backflow of blood. Aortic and pulmonary valves collectively called as semilunar (SL) valves are moon shaped, located at the base of both the pulmonary trunk (pulmonary artery) and the aorta and permits blood to be forced into the arteries, but prevent backflow of blood from the arteries into the ventricles

Systemic and pulmonary circulation

Systemic circulation : This involves flow of oxygenated blood from left ventricle into aorta though the SL valves, then into arteries, arterioles and finally into the systemic capillaries in which exchange of gases and nutrients take place. Blood unloads oxygen and takes up carbon dioxide though capillaries and venules and the same travel towards right atrium of heart from veins and the process continues.

Pulmonary circulation : During ventricular diastole (ventricular relaxation), deoxygenated blood from the right ventricle flows into the pulmonary trunk, which branches into pulmonary arteries that carry blood towards the lungs. In pulmonary capillaries, deoxygenated blood transports carbon dioxide into the alveoli of the lungs which is exhaled (outside the body) and oxygen is inhaled. The oxygenated blood flows into pulmonary veins and then into the left atrium. Through the left atrium, it flows into left ventricle via bicuspid (AV) valve.

Coronary circulation : It is the circulation within the heart blood vessels (coronary arteries) which supplies the oxygenated blood to the myocardium. The coronary arteries branch from the ascending aorta and encircle the heart. During contraction, a small amount of blood flows into the coronary arteries because they are squeezed shut. When the heart is filling with blood (during relaxation), the high pressure in aorta propels blood through coronary arteries, into capillaries and then coronary veins.

Coronary arteries : The left and right coronary arteries branch from the ascending aorta and supply oxygenated blood to the myocardium (cardiac muscle). The left artery divides into left anterior descending artery (an anterior interventricular sulcus supplies oxygenated blood to the walls of both ventricles) and circumflex branches (supplies oxygenated blood to the walls of left ventricle and atrium). The right coronary artery supplies blood to the right atrium and divides into posterior interventricular branches (supplies oxygenated blood to the walls of both ventricles) and marginal branches (transports oxygenated blood to the right ventricle only).

Coronary veins : From the coronary arteries, blood flows into capillaries, which supply oxygen and nutrients to each and every cell and transports carbon dioxide and nitrogenous wastes to the excretory organs such as the skin, lungs and kidneys. The deoxygenated blood from myocardium drains into vascular sinus of the coronary sulcus on the posterior surface of the heart coronary and this blood further drains into the right atrium.

Conduction system

Heart beats due to its inherent and rhythmic electrical activity. Autorhythmic fibers are responsible for such activity; they repeatedly generate an action potential due to which the heart muscles contract.

Autorhythmic fibers : These act as pacemaker and form the conduction system-a specialised network of cardiac muscle fibers, gives direction for each cycle of cardiac excitation to progress thorough the heart consisting of the following sequences

(a) SA Node- situated in the right atrial wall just inferior to the opening of the superior vena cava, from where the excitation begins. The SA nodal cells spontaneously depolarize as they do not have stable resting potential; and thereby produce pacemaker potential. When pacemaker potential reaches to threshold, it triggers an action potential and thus the atria contract. SA node initiates action potential 100 times per minute and is greater than any node because of action potential propagates throughout the conduction system through this node.

(b) AV node : The action potential conducted through the SA node, reaches AV node in the septum between two atria, near the opening of coronary sinus.

(c) Bundle of His-From AV node, the action potential enters the AV bundle and propagates towards the ventricle.

(d) Bundle branches-Action potential from bundle of His enters the right and left bundle branches, which extends through interventricular septum towards the apex of the heart.

(e) Purkinje fibers-The purkinje fibers rapidly conduct action potential from apex of the heart to the remainder of the ventricular myocardium which results in ventricular contraction, pushing the blood towards semilunar valves.

Cardiac cycle

Events occuring during each beat of heart is called as cardiac cycle. In each cardiac cycle, there is alternative contraction and relaxation of heart, forcing blood from high pressure areas to low pressure areas. At normal heart rate (72 beats/min), each cardiac cycle is for about 0.8 sec. Following are the events that occur during each cardiac cycle.

Atrial systole : As the atria contract, the ventricles relax. Atrial systole due to depolarisation of SA node, is suggested by 'P' wave in electrocardiogram (ECG) and lasts for about 0.1 sec. Due to contraction of atria, nearly about 25 ml of blood moves into the ventricles through the AV valve. At atrial systole, 25 ml blood along with 105 ml which is present in the ventricles contribute a total of 130 ml of blood volume which is the end diastolic volume (end of relaxation) and appears as QRS complex further suggesting onset of ventricular depolarisation.

Ventricular systole : During ventricular contraction, atria relax simultaneously (atrial diastole) building up the pressure in the ventricles and pushes blood up against AV valves forcing them to close. The time during which both the SL and AV valves are closed for period of 0.05 sec is called as isovolumetric contraction. As the ventricles contract, pressure in left ventricle exceeds the pressure in the aorta by 80 mm hg and pressure in the right ventricle is greater than the pressure in the pulmonary trunk by 20 mm Hg. This causes both SL valves to open (ventricular ejection) ejecting about 70 ml of blood from left ventricle into aorta and from the right ventricle into the pulmonary trunk. The volume that remains in each ventricle at the time of ventricular systole is called end systolic volume (60 ml). The volume ejected during each beat from the ventricles, is known as stoke volume which equals the end diastolic minus end systolic volume

$$EDV (130ml) - ESV (60ml) = SV (70 ml)$$

Ventricular diastole : During ventricular relaxation, there is less pressure in the ventricles, so that blood flows back into ventricles form aorta and pulmonary trunk allowing SL valves to close; there is brief interval after closing of SL valves. When ventricular blood volume does not change because all four valves are closed, this period is called isovolumetric relaxation. The atrial pressure is directly influenced by the cardiac output (SV × HR) and the peripheral resistance (resistance which the wall of arterioles exerts on the blood flow.)

The important factors regulating blood pressure include total peripheral resistance, heart rate, myocardial contractility, and venous return.

Pathophysiological significance

Hypertension- Persistence elevation of blood pressure above 120/80 mm of Hg.

Glomerulonephritis : Any cause which leads to obstruction of renal blood flow causing release of renin in the blood. High renin in blood produces vasoconstriction and thus high blood pressure.

Hyperaldosteronism : Results in excess reabsorption of Na^+ ions and water leading to increase in volume of body fluid.

Pheochormocytoma : Tumour of adrenal gland causes continues release of adrenaline and thereby blood pressure is increased due to increased heart rate and force of contraction.

Myocarditis : Also known as inflammatory cardiomyopathy, it is the inflammation of heart muscle. Symptoms of myocarditis are fatigue, chest pain, irregular beating, and pain of joints.

Stenosis- narrowing of heart valve opening which restricts blood flow.

Mitral stenosis : Scar formation or congenital defect results in narrowing of bicuspid valve.

Myocardial ischemia : Partial obstruction of blood flow in the coronary arteries

Myocardial infarction (MI) : Complete obstruction to blood flow in coronary arteries.

2. BLOOD VESSELS

Blood vessels are of five types consisting of arteries, arterioles, capillaries, venules and veins.

Arteries : Arteries carry oxygenated blood away from heart to other organs. Arteries consist of three layers of tissue. Outer layer consists of fibrous tissue called as tunica adventitia, middle layer consists of smooth muscle and elastic tissue called tunica media and the inner lining consists of squamous epithelium called as endothelium.

Arterioles : Medium sized arteries divide into small arteries, which in turn divide into still smaller arteries called as arterioles. Arterioles are abundant microscopic vessels that regulate the flow of blood into the capillary network of the body's tissue. Arterioles also consist of layers similar to that of arteries. The diameter of arterioles is 15 μm-300 μm. The terminal end of arterioles called as metarteriole, which narrows toward capillary junction and thus forms pre-capillary sphincter, which monitors the flow of blood into the capillary.

Capillaries : The larger branches of arterioles entering into tissues are called as capillaries which form hair like network. These are the smallest blood vessels with a diameter of 5-10 μm and composed of a single layer of endothelial cells. The exchange of substances between blood and tissues take place through capillaries only. The flow of blood from metarteriole through capillaries and into post capillary venule is called as microcirculation. It forms a link between arterioles and venules.

Venules : Numerous capillaries within a tissue reunite forming venules. Venules have a diameter of 10-50 μm and have thin walls. Venules brings the deoxygenated blood from capillaries towards veins and finally to the heart.

Veins : Venules merge to form larger blood vessels known as veins. Veins bring blood from the tissues back to the heart. Veins have very thin walls relative to their total diameter because there is less muscle and elastic tissue in tunic media. The diameter ranges from 0.5 to 3 cm. Some veins possess valves, which prevent the back flow of blood. The valves are formed by a fold of tunica intima strengthened by connective tissues.

EXERCISE

1. Discuss in brief, the anatomy of the heart.
2. Describe the layers of the heart.
3. Give the physiology of heart chambers.
4. Define systemic, pulmonary and coronary circulation.
5. Enlist various valves and give their role.
6. Describe cardiac cycle.
7. Give the events occuring during cardiac cycle.
8. What is blood pressure (BP)? Enlist the factors responsible for high BP.
9. Discuss the conduction system of the heart.
10. Enlist various blood vessels.
11. Give the functioning of the capillaries
12. Give the layers of the blood vessels.

❖❖❖

EXPERIMENT NO. 25

STUDY OF THE DIGESTIVE SYSTEM

➢ Aim

To study the human digestive system.

➢ Theory

Digestion is the process of breakdown of food into small molecules and the various organs involved in digestion collectively form the digestive system. The digestive system comprises of gastrointestinal (GI) tract (mouth, pharynx, esophagus, stomach and small and large intestine) and accessory digestive organs (teeth, tongue. salivary glands, liver, gall bladder and pancreas) as shown in the figure 25.1

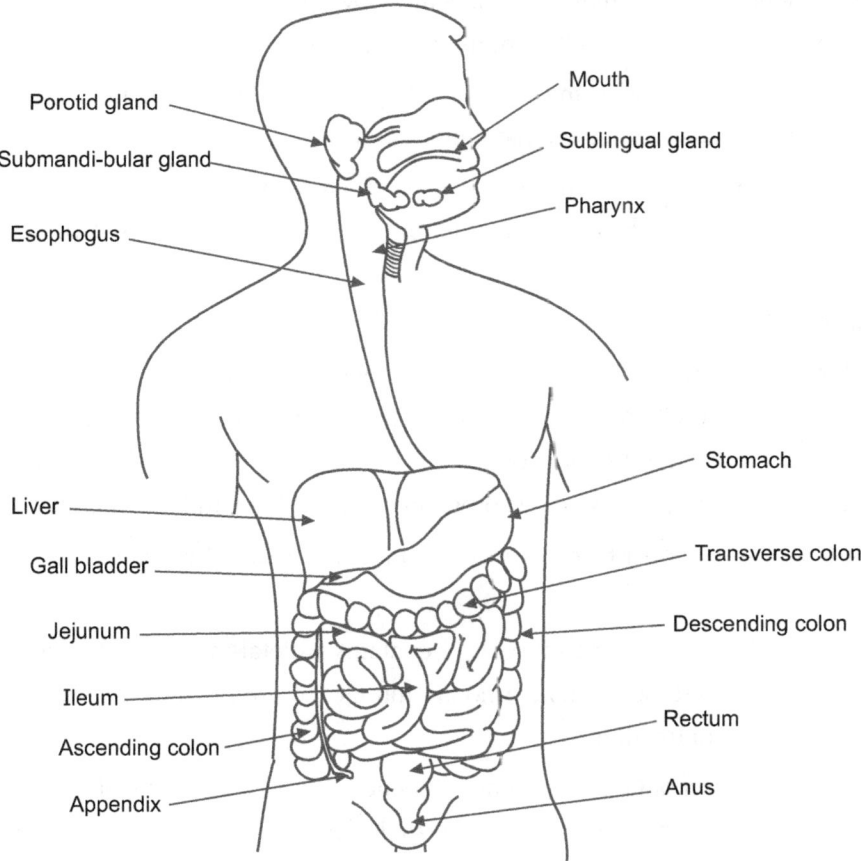

Figure 25.1 : Digestive system

Various processes performed by the digestive system are enumerated below.

1. **Ingestion/eating :** Taking food and liquids into the mouth for digestion or absorption.

2. **Secretion :** GI tract and accessory digestive organs secrete about 7 liters of water, buffers and enzymes per day into the digestive system.

3. **Mixing and propulsion :** Spontaneous contraction and relaxation of smooth muscles of GI tract, mixes the food and secretions and pushes them toward the rectum. This propulsion of GI due to contraction and relaxation along its length is called mobility of the GI.

4. **Digestion :** Breakdown of food (carbohydrate, protein by hydrolysis) into smaller and simpler molecules mechanically by peristaltic action and enzymatic breakdown facilitated by the churning action and enzymes.

5. **Absorption :** Transfers ingested food/liquids into the epithelial cells (muscular, submucosal layer) and then into blood circulation.

6. **Defecation :** Indigested material, wastes, microorganisms slogged off from GI tract lining leave the body through rectum in the form of feces by the process known as defecation.

Layers of the GI tract

(a) **Mucosa :** Innermost layer of the GI tract, mucosal layer is in direct contact with the contents of the GI and is composed of epithelium, lamina propia, areolar muscular mucosa (smooth muscle), connective tissue with blood and lymphatic vessels, through which nutrients are absorbed from the GI tract and then circulated.

(b) **Submucosa :** Consists of areolar connective tissue that binds mucosa to the muscularis.

(c) **Muscularis :** Much of the muscularis contains skeletal muscle that allows voluntary swallowing and defecation. Smooth muscles of muscularis are responsible for involuntary contraction.

(d) **Serosa :** Portion of GI tract that are suspended in the abdominopelvic cavity. This is also called as visceral peritoneum as it forms a part of the peritoneum. The functioning of the GI tract is regulated by enteric and autonomic (self governing) nervous system.

(e) **Peritoneum (Peritoneal cavity)** : It is the largest serous membrane of the body. The space between parietal (abdominopelvic) and visceral portion containing serous fluid is called peritoneal cavity.

Organs of the GI tract

(a) **Mouth/oral cavity** : Tongue, cheeks and hard and soft palates constitute the parts of the mouth. Opening of mouth is the lips which help to keep the food between upper and lower teeth during mastication (chewing).

(b) **Pharynx** : Food when swallowed, passes from the mouth into pharynx and laryngopharynx (part of pharynx) and due to contraction, food is propelled into the esophagus.

(c) **Esophagus** : It is a 25 cm collapsible muscular tube, that lies posterior to the trachea. It has three layers, mucosa, submucosa and serosa. Muscularis forms two sphincters; the upper esophageal sphincter, regulates food movement from pharynx to esophagus and lower esophageal sphincter, regulates food movement from esophagus to stomach. Esophagus does not have serosa, instead it has adventia, which attaches the esophagus to the surrounding structure. The main function of esophagus is to secrete mucus and transport food into the stomach.

(d) **Stomach** : It is the elongated pouch like part of the digestive canal which is a 'J' shaped structure that lies below the diaphragm (figure 25.2). The size of the stomach varies due to presence and absence of foods. After ingestion of food, the size increases because of wall enlargement and as the food passes into the intestine, walls partially collapse. It normally accommodates liquids upto a volume of 1.1.5 liters. Stomach lies in the upper part of abdominal cavity and connects the esophagus to the intestine (duodenum). The position of stomach due to excessive food ingestion or intake gets distended largely due to which it interferes with the descent of the diaphragm, causing dysprea upon inspiration (difficulties in breathing). The cardia, fundus, body and pylorus are the four divisions of the stomach. The cardia surrounds the superior opening of the stomach. The fundus is the enlarged portion to the left and is superior to the cardia. The body is the central part of the stomach. The pylorus is the part which connects the stomach to the duodenum and regulates the content through the pyloric sphincter. The two curvatures of the stomach are 1) Lesser curvature : which is formed by the upper right surface (concave part) and 2) Greater curvature : formed by the lower left surface (convex part). The epithelial linings of stomach form a large numbers of folds called rugae .Depression in the rugae are called the gastric pits. Inferior to the gastric pits are numerous columns of secretary cells called as gastric glands which secrete their content (gastric juice with HCl) into the stomach. Gastric glands and mucus neck cells secret mucus, parietal cells produce intrinsic factor needed for vitamin B12 absorption and chief cells secret pepsinogen and gastric lipase. The gastric juice is the sum of secretion from these glands, which totals 1.5-3 liters/day.

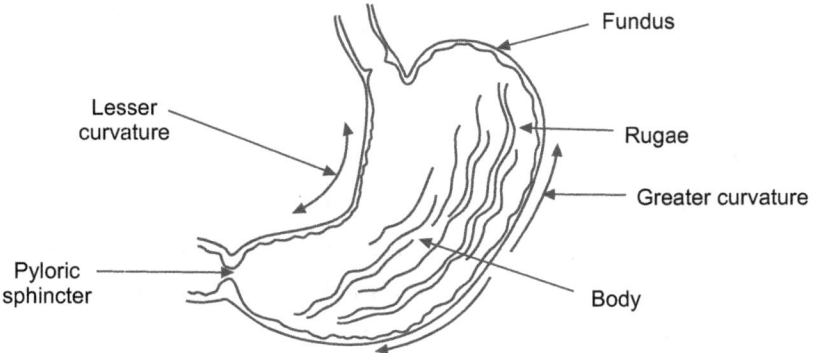

Figure 25.2 : Stomach

After ingestion of food, gentle rippling, and peristaltic movements in stomach called mixing waves pass over the stomach every 20-25 sec. These waves macerate food, mix it with gastric secretion, forming a soupy liquid called 'chyme'. During chyme formation, nearly about 2-3 ml of this is forced periodically through partially closed pyloric sphincter into the duodenum and this process is called as gastric emptying. The functions of stomach includes : reservoir for food storage until its passage into the intestine, secretion of gastric juice and gastrin for digestion, absorption of drugs, water etc, secretion of HCl which kills the many microbes present in ingested foods.

(e) **Small intestine :** The small intestine is called so, because of its small diameter (2.5 cm), however, its length is longer (nearly about 6 meters) than that of the large intestine. It consists of duodenum, jejunum and ileum. The duodenum (25 cm long), is the anterior part of small intestine to which the pyloric region of the stomach is joined. The duodenum becomes jejunum at the point where the tube turns abruptly forward and downward. The middle of small intestine called jejunum (2.5 cm) joins to the terminal part of the ileum (3.5 cm). Numerous tiny projections called villi are present on the intestinal lining and each villi consists of arterioles, venules and lymph vessels. Epithelial cells present on villi have brush like surface called brush border. There are numerous microvilli on each border. These villi and microvilli increase the surface area of the small intestine so that maximum digestion and absorption take place. Small intestinal mucosa has a number of deep crevices (a narrow opening or fissure) lined with glandular epithelium which form the intestinal glands and secrete juice. Other cells found on intestinal lining are the paneth cells which secrete lysozyme, and entero-endocrine cells; S cells which secrete secretine, K cells which secrete cholecystokinin and glucose dependent insulinotorpic peptide (GLP).

(f) **Large intestine :** It is the terminal part of the GI tract, and called large intestine due to its diameter (6.5) which is greater than that of the small intestine and is about 1.5 meter long. Large intestine has 4 major regions mainly, cecum, colon, rectum and anus. Regulation of movement of contents from the small to large intestine is controlled by ileocecal sphincter. Adjacent to ileocecal junction, is a blind pouch called cecum. Appendix attached to cecum, is a coiled tube structure and is also called as vermiform appendix. Colon- the merging of cecum into the food passage is called colon, which is further sub divided as ascending colon (vertically moved on the right side of the abdomen, reaches to the lower border of liver), transverse colon (passes horizontally across the abdomen, below the liver, stomach and spleen) descending colon (down side of abdomen) and sigmoid colon (last portion of large intestine which is below the iliac creast). Rectum- the end part of GI tract which lies anterior to the sacrum and coccyx. Anus - the terminal 2-3 cm of rectum is the anal canal and opening of this canal to the exterior is called as the anus.

The wall of the large intestine shows the presence of intestinal mucus glands which secrete lubricating fluid, which coats the feces as they are formed. The longitudinal muscle is grouped into tape like strips called teniae coli and the circular muscles are grouped into pouch like haustra between them.

(g) **Salivary glands :** Three pairs of gland (parotids, submandibulars and sublingual) secrete a major volume of saliva produced everyday. The buccal gland, located in the lining of mucosa of the cheeks and mouth contribute less towards salivary secretion. Salivary glands located outside of alimentary canal releases its secretion into the lumen of GI tract for digestion of ingested food.

(h) **Liver :** The largest gland of the body, the liver is reddish brown in colour, located in the upper part of abdominal cavity occupying the right hypochondriac region, the greater part of epogastium, reaching into the left *hypochondrium*. Organs adjacent to liver : superiorly and inferiorly are listed as follows

Inferiorly- stomach, duodenum, right kidney,

Posteriorly-esophagus, inferior vena cava, aorta, gall bladder and vertebral column,

Laterally-lower ribs and diaphragm.

Liver is enclosed in a thin inelastic capsule and coved by the peritoneum. It is tightly held by supporting ligaments and pressure of the organs in the abdominal cavity. The liver has four lobes- right, left and caudate quadrates. The important functions of liver are given below.

(i) Metabolism of carbohydrates, proteins and fats

(ii) Synthesis of bile and prothrombin,

(iii) Excretion of drugs, toxins, poisons, cholesterols and bile pigments etc,

(iv) Inactivation of hormones (mainly insulin, glucagon, cortisol etc),

(v) Heat production, and

(vi) Storage of glycogen, fat soluble vitamins, iron, copper etc.

(i) **Gallbladder :** A pear shaped sac attached posteriorly to the liver, having fundus, body and neck as the main regions. The main function is storage and release of bile into bile duct and then into the duodenum.

(j) **Pancreas :** Leaf shaped structure, pale gray in colour weighing 60 gm and located in the epigastric region of the abdominal cavity. Pancreas acts as both exocrine and endocrine gland as 99 % of its secretion is exocrine i.e. pancreatic juice secreted into the duodenum through hepatopancreatic ampula and 1 % constitutes the endocrine secretion i.e. secretion of hormones (insulin, glucagon and somatostatin) directly into blood circulation.

➢ Pathological significance

- **Nausea**

  Sensation of vomiting.

- **Vomiting (emesis)**

  It is the forceful expulsion of the content of stomach through the mouth.

- **Gastro esophageal reflux disorder (GERD)**

  Dysfunction of the lower esophageal sphincter in which the contents of stomach reflux (flow backwards) into the esophagus leading to the irritation of the lining of the esophagus.

- **Reflux Esophagitis**

  Inflammation of the esophagus because of reflux of acidic contents of the stomach.

- **Heartburn**

  A burning sensation in a region near the heart due to irritation of the mucosa of the esophagus due to acidic contents of the stomach.

- **Jaundice**

  It is a disorder of the GI system characterised by yellowish colouration of eyes, skin, and mucous membranes due to excessive release of bilurubin from liver.

- **Hepatitis**

  It is the inflammation of liver caused due to viral infection, drugs, alcohol and chemicals.

- **Diarrhea**

  It is an increase in frequency, volume and fluid content of the feces due to intestinal hyper motility.

- **Constipation**

  It is infrequent or difficult defecation (passing of feces) caused due to reduced motility of intestine.

EXERCISE

1. What is digestion? Enlist the various parts of the digestive system.
2. Draw and label the digestive system.
3. Discuss the various processes performed by the digestive system.
4. Enlist parts of the gastrointestinal system.
5. Describe the anatomy and physiology of stomach
6. Describe the anatomy of the liver.
7. Enlist the various functions of the liver.
8. Define the following terms-
   (a) Nausea,
   (b) Vomiting,
   (c) GERD,
   (d) Jaundice,
   (e) Hepatitis,
   (f) Heartburn,
   (g) Constipation,
   (h) Diarrhea.

❖❖❖

EXPERIMENT NO. 26

STUDY OF THE RESPIRATORY SYSTEM

➢ **Aim**

To study the human respiratory system.

➢ **Theory**

The functioning of the respiratory system along with the circulatory system is essential for the exchange of oxygen and carbon dioxide (gases). Respiration is the chemical process in the biological system where in exchange of these gases take place (cellular respiration is the constant supply of oxygen to cells for energy-conversion process that occur in the mitochondria of the cells). The exchange of gases between blood and the lungs is called external respiration, while the exchange between blood and the cells is called internal respiration.

Anatomically, the respiratory system has two parts viz. upper respiratory tract (nose, nasopharynx, oropharynx, laryngopharynx and larynx); lower respiratory tract (trachea, bronchial tree including, bronchioles, alveolar ducts, alveolar sac and alveoli) (figure 26.1)

Physiologically, respiratory system includes various accessory parts, oral cavity, rib cage and respiratory muscles (diaphragm).

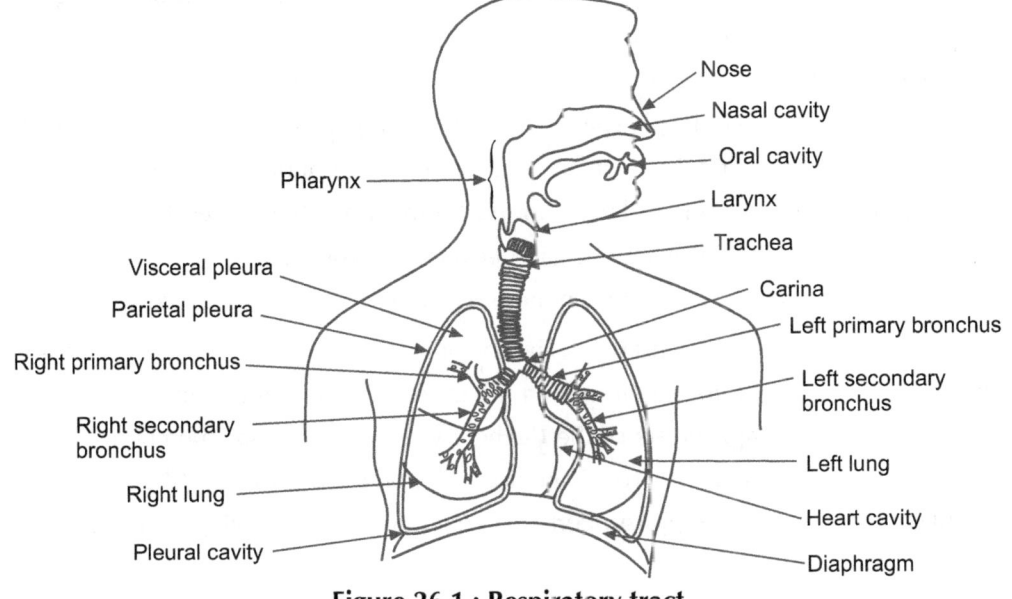

Figure 26.1 : Respiratory tract

➤ Upper respiratory tract

(a) Nose : It is divided into external and internal structures. External structure consists of supporting framework of bone and hyaline cartilage which surrounds the muscle and skin. The nose is surrounded by maxilla laterally and inferiorly at its base. The flaring cartilaginous expansion forming and supporting the outer side of each oval nostril opening is called as the ala. The nasal passage of internal nose lies on the roof of the mouth. The nasal passage is separated into right and left cavity by a middle portion called as the septum. In side the nasal cavity, the frontal region is known as vestibule. The nasal passage consists of pseudo stratified ciliated columnar epithelium cells. The olfactory receptors (for smell sensation) are situated on lining of the superior nasal conchae and near the septum. The functions of the nose include-warming of inhaled air and entrapment of particulate matter and bacteria in the sticky mucous.

(b) Pharynx : It is also known as throat. It is funnel shaped, up to 13-14 cm long and lined by mucus membrane. Fibrous and mucus tissues begin at the internal half and extend to the cricoids and inferior cartilage of the larynx. The pharynx lies posterior to the nasal and oral cavities, superior to the larynx and just anterior to the cervical vertebrae and forms the common passage for food and air, and provides a resonating chamber for voice production. It is divided into nasopharynx, oropharynx and laryngopharynx.

(c) Larynx : The larynx is known as the voice box, located between the root of tongue and upper end of trachea and in front of the lower part of the pharynx. The shape of larynx is triangular with attachment of cartilages to one another by ligaments. The cavity of larynx extends from its triangle shaped inlet at the epiglottis to the circular outlet at the lower border of the cricoids cartilage, where it is continuous with the lumen of the trachea. The pairs of folds of larynx form 3 compartments viz. vestibular, vocal and lower true vocal cords. The slit like gap between the true vocal cords is called as rima glottidis. Glottis is the space between the rima glottidis and true vocal cords.

(d) Trachea : The trachea or wind pipe is a tubular structure, 11-12 cm long, extends from the larynx in the neck to the bronchi in the thoracic cavity and divided into right and left bronchi. The major layers of the tracheal walls are mucosa, submucosa, hyaline, cartilage and adventitia. The 16-20 incomplete, horizontal rings of 'C' shaped hyaline cartilage provide a semi rigid support and hence prevent the collapse of tracheal wall during inhalation.

(e) The bronchi : The right and left bronchi begin at the level of the 5th thoracic vertebra. The right bronchus is vertical, shorter and wider that the left one. Carnia is the internal ring, from where trachea divides into right and left bronchus. The mucus membrane of the carnia is the susceptible part of the larynx and trachea involved in cough reflex. After entering into the right lung, the right divides into 3 branches while the left bronchus after entering into the left lung, divides into two branches, one goes to each lobe of the lung. Each branch then divides into bronchioles and subdivides into smaller bronchioles. Bronchi are lined with ciliated columnar epithelial cells and the terminally bronchi are lined with simple cuboidal epithelium. The bronchioles are divided into alveolar ducts, and these ducts result in the formation of bag like structures known as alveoli which are responsible for the exchange of gases. The main functions of bronchi are adhering to foreign particulates and bacteria due to their sticky nature and the movement of mucus towards the throat.

(f) The lung : The lung is a cone shaped organ located in the thoracic cavity, that extends from the diaphragm to a point slightly above the clavicles. Heart and other adjacent organs in the mediatstinum, separates the thoracic cavity into structurally different chambers. Pleural membranes protect the lungs from any damage. The superficial layer called the parietal pleura, lines the wall of the thoracic cavity, deeper layer known as visceral pleura, covers the lungs. Pleural cavity is the space between the parietal and visceral pleurae which contains a lubricating fluid, which aids in reduction of friction between membranes. Due to the space occupied by the heart, the left lung is about 10 % smaller that right lung. The main and important function of lungs is the exchange of gases.

> **Physiology of respiratory system**

Respiration is a process by which the lungs inhale the air in and thereby expand the size and contract to exhale air.

> **Phases of respiration**

When the capacity of the thoracic cavity is increased by contraction of intercostal muscles and diaphragm, pressure in the thoracic cavity decreases as compared to the atmospheric pressure. These results in air being drawn into the lungs to equalise the alveolar and atmospheric pressure in the process called inspiration or inhalation.

When the diaphragm and intercostal muscles relax, the ribs regain their original position, the diaphragm ascends, and the lungs recoil and this results expiration or exhalation. There is a brief pause (stoppage of breathing) and another cycle begins.

➤ Pathological significance

Pharyngitis : It is the inflammation of pharynx.

Laryngitis : It is the inflammation of larynx.

Asthma : It is a disorder characterised by obstruction in airway, inflammation, hypersensitivity which causes difficulties in breathing. These symptoms may be due to release of chemical substances, histamine, bradykinin and leukotrienes (inflammatory mediators) in response to antigenic stimuli.

Chronic obstructive pulmonary diseases (COPD) : These diseases are characterised by persistent airway obstruction due to emphysema or bronchitis.

Chronic bronchitis : Chronic bronchitis presents itself as cough with or without expectoration for at least 3-4 months of a year for 2 consecutive years.

Emphysema : It is the enlargement of alveoli with destruction of alveolar septa.

Pneumonia : It is an infectious disease characterised by alveolar inflammation, fever, chills productive or dry cough, malaise (pain throughout body) and chest pain. *Streptococcus pneumonia* is the common causative microorganism responsible for the pneumonia but it can also be caused by viruses, fungi and parasites.

Tuberculosis : It is an infectious and communicable disease caused due *to Mycobacterium tuberculosis* affecting lungs and pleurae of bronchi, and it is characterised by symptoms mainly fatigue, loss of weight and appetite, cough, chest pain etc.

EXERCISE

1. What is respiration? Differentiate between external and internal respiration.
2. Enlists the organs of upper and lower respiratory tracts.
3. Give the anatomy of bronchi.
4. Explain the physiology of respiration.
5. What is asthma and pneumonia?

EXPERIMENT NO. 27

STUDY OF THE URINARY SYSTEM

➢ Aim

To study the human urinary system

➢ Theory

Urinary system is the system responsible for the elimination and excretion. Kidneys are the major organs of the urinary system.

Urinary system consists of two kidneys for urine formation, two ureters for passage of urine from kidneys to urinary bladder, one urinary bladder for temporary collection and storage of urine, and one urethra for discharge of urine (figure 27.1). Urinary system along with urine formation, also balances the blood plasma so that the hemostasis or dynamic constancy of internal fluid environment is maintained.

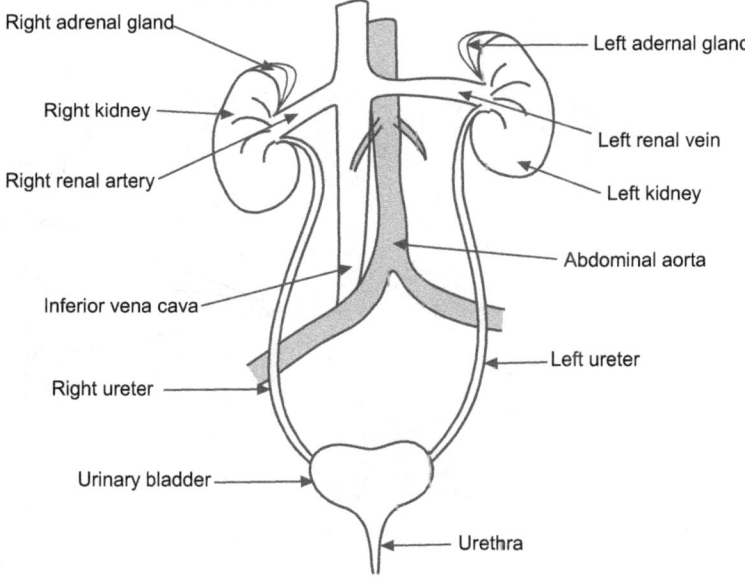

Figure 27.1 : Organs of the Urinary System

➢ Organs of the urinary system

(a) Kidney : A kidney is a bean shaped organ, 10-12 cm long, 5-7 cm wide and 3 cm thick and weighing 130-150 gm. It is a retroperitoneal (behind the peritoneum) organ as it is positioned posteriorly to the peritoneal cavity. Kidneys are located between the levels of last thoracic and third lumbar vertebrae. The left kidney is often larger that the right. A heavy cushion of fat normally encloses kidneys for maintaining its position. The medial surface of each kidney has a concave notch called as hilum through which the ureters emerge. Internally, a kidney consists of an outer region called the renal cortex, an inner region called the renal medulla. The medulla contains medullary pyramids (figure 27.2). The tip of each pyramid empties urine into a minor calyx, which in turn empties into a major calyx. The number of calyces join together to form larger collection reservoir knows as renal pelvis that becomes the ureter, once it leaves the hilum of kidney. Each kidney contains millions of nephorns which are involved in urine formation. The nephron is the structural and functional unit of the kidney. Each nephron consists of two parts: renal corpuscles where blood plasma is filtered and renal tubule into which the filtered fluid passes. Renal corpuscles have two components i.e. glomerulus and glomerular capsule (Bowman's capsule). The renal tubule consists of proximal convoluted tubule (PCT), loop of Henle and distal convoluted tubule (DCT). The DCT empties into the collecting duct.

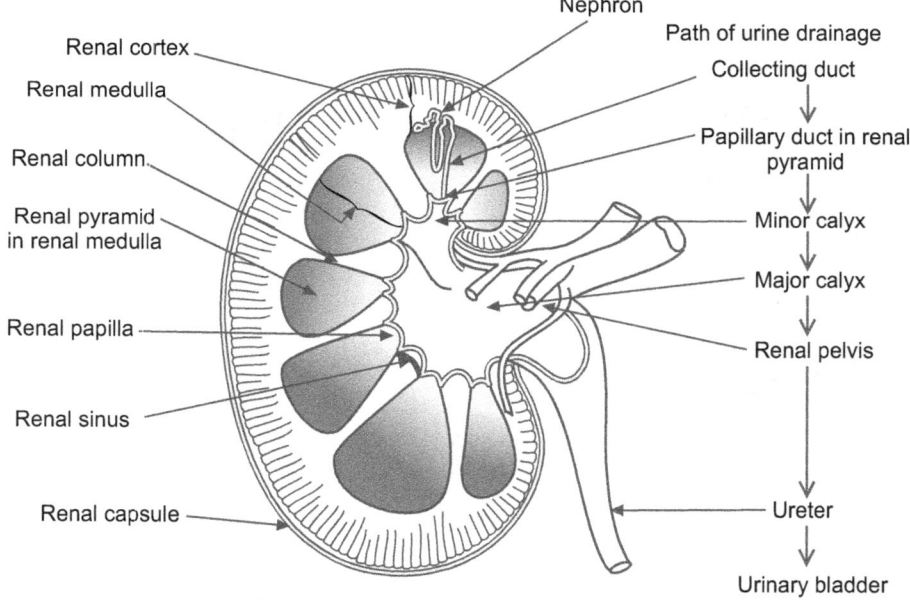

Figure 27.2: Kidney

> **Functions of the kidney**

1. Regulation of blood pH and ionic composition of the blood (mainly Na^+, K^+, Ca^{2+}, Cl^- and PO_4^-),

2. Regulation of blood volume and pressure,

3. Maintenance of blood osmolarity,
4. Production of hormones like calcitriol and erythropoietin for calcium homeostasis and RBC production respectively,
5. Blood glucose regulation, by synthesis of glucose from amino acids,
6. Excretion of wastes and foreign substances etc.

(b) Ureters : Two ureters are tubes acting as a passage for urine towards urinary bladder from the kidneys. Each ureter is continuous with the funnel shaped pelvis of the kidney. Each ureter measures 25-30 cm, are thick walled narrow tubes with 1-10 mm diameter along their course between the renal pelvis and urinary bladder. Each ureter passes down through the abdominal cavity and opens into posterior aspects of the base of the urinary bladder. It has 3 layers mainly, fibrous tissues, muscular tissues and mucous layer. The muscular tissue propels the urine by peristalsis. The rate and strength of peristalsis increases with increasing urine volume.

(c) Urinary bladder : It is a hollow, distensible, muscular, pear shape organ situated in the pelvic cavity and is posterior to the pubic symphysis and thus it is acts as a reservoir for urine. The size and shape of the bladder depends upon the amount of urine it contains. The smooth muscle of the wall of the bladder is called as detrusor muscle. There are 3 openings in the floor of the bladder-two from the ureter and one in the urethra. The ureter openings lie at the posterior portion and the urethral openings at the anterior, lower corner.

(d) Urethra : It is a small canal that extends from the neck of the urinary bladder, in the female. The urethra lies behind the symphysis pubis and is anterior to the vagina In male, the urethra passes through center of the prostate gland. As the male urethra is joined by the ejaculatory duct, it serves as a pathway for semen also. Therefore, urethra is part of urinary as well as reproductive system of the male. The female urethra is separate from the vagina (reproductive system part), which lies just behind the urethra.

➤ Process of urine formation

- **Glomerular filtration :** It is the movement of water and solutes in blood plasma across the walls of glomerular capillaries into the glomerular capsules and finally into the renal tubules.

- **Tubular reabsorption :** As the filtered fluid flows along with the renal tubule and through the collecting duct, tubule cells reabsorb about 99 % of the filtered water and many useful solutes. The water and solutes return to the blood as it flows through the peritubular capillaries and vasa recta.

- **Tubular secretion :** It is the movement of molecules out of the peritubular blood and into the tubules for excretion.

  Composition of urine : Urine consists of 95 % water and 5 % of the other components which includes urea, uric acid, ammonia, creatinine, and ions (Na^+, K^+, NH_3^-, Cl^-, HCO_3^-, PO_4^-, SO_4 etc).

> **Pathological significance**

Urinary tract infection : Colonisation and multiplication of microorganisms (bacteria, viruses fungi or parasites)results in infection. This infection is largely observed in females due to shorter urethra and lack of bactericidal prostatic fluids.

Cystitis : It is the inflammation of urinary bladder due to infection and is often observed in females mainly during the reproductive age. The organisms present in the vagina during sexual intercourse can travel to the urethra. Symptoms include pain, burning sensation on urination, urine with pus or blood etc.

Renal failure : It is the dysfunction of the urinary system. Renal failure may be acute or chronic. In acute renal failure, a sudden and usually reversible deterioration of renal function results in accumulation of metabolic waste products, where as chronic renal failure is a permanent decrement in glomerular filtration rate due to parenchymal distraction.

Glomerulonephritis : It is the inflammation of glomeruli and may result in chronic renal failure

EXERCISE

1. Enlist the various parts of the kidney along with their functions.
2. Describe the anatomy of the kidney.
3. Enumerate the functions of the kidney.
4. Describe the process of urine formation
5. Discuss the following terms--
   (a) Urinary tract infection,
   (b) Glomerulonephritis,
   (c) Cystitis,
   (d) Renal failure.

EXPERIMENT NO. 28

STUDY OF THE HUMAN SKULL

➢ Aim

To study the human skull

➢ Theory

The human skeleton is made up of 206 bones and is divided as axial and appendicular skeleton. The axial skeleton consists of bones arranged along the axis which include the skull bones, ear bones, hyoid bone, ribs, breast bones, and back bones. The appendicular skeleton consists of the bones of the upper and lower limbs and the bones forming the girdles that connect the limbs of the axial skeleton.

➢ The skull

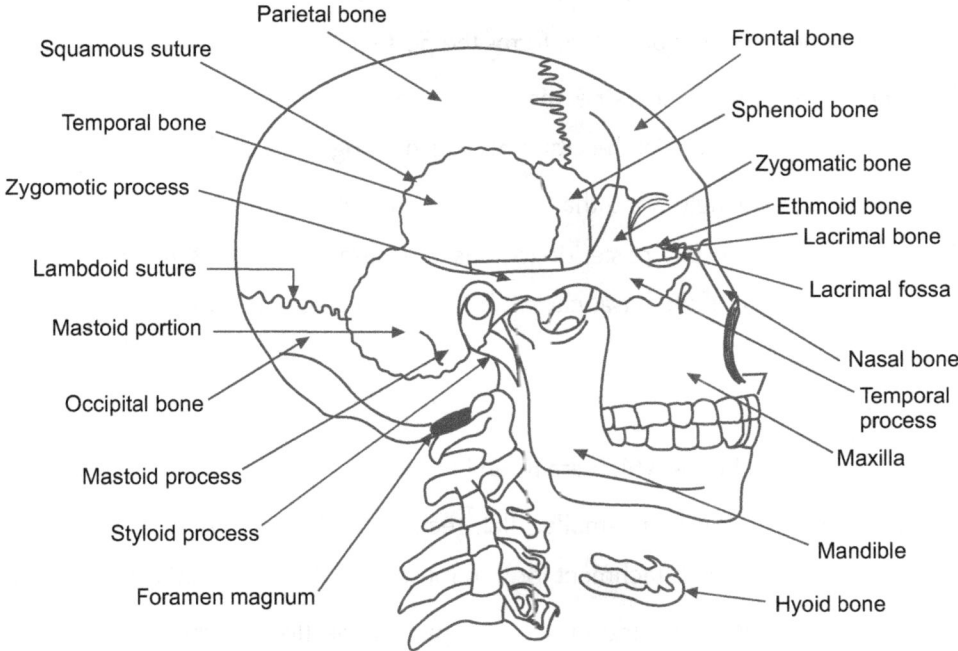

Figure 28.1 : Skull showing facial and cranial bones with hyoid bone

The skull is bony framework (figure 28.1) of the head having nearly 22 bones that rests on the superior end of the vertebral column. Skull bones are categorized into a) Cranial Bones, and b) Facial Bones

(A) Cranial Bones :

Cranial bones form the cranium which offers protection to the brain.

They are eight in number and their description is given below:

- **Frontal bone :** A single bone that forms the anterior part of the forehead, roof of the orbit and most of anterior part of the cranial floor.
- **Parietal bones :** Two in number that forms the middle part of the skull. Inner side contains blood vessels that supply blood to the dura matter of the brain
- **Temporal bones :** Two bones that form the inferior lateral part of the cranium. An inferior projection of the temporal part is called as zygomatic process,
- **Occipital bone :** A single bone that forms the posterior and basal part of the skull.
- **Sphenoid bone :** A single bone that lies at the middle part of the skull. It tightly articulates all other bones of the cranium, thus holding them all together.
- **Ethmoid bone :** A single bone that forms the anterior part of the cranium. Anterior to this is the sphenoid and posterior to it is the nasal bone. It is the major superior supporting structure of the nasal cavity and forms an extensive surface area of the nasal cavity.

(B) Facial Bones :

There are 14 facial bones which are listed below.

- **Two nasal bones :** These are smaller, flat, rectangular bones forming the bridge of the nose. These bones offer attachment for thin muscles that take part in facial expression.
- **Two maxillas :** They form the upper jaw, part of the floor of the orbits, part of the lateral walls of nasal cavity as well as hard plate (bony roof of mouth). On each side, maxilla has maxillary sinus that empties into the nasal cavity. The alveolar process of the *maxillae* holds the upper teeth, and is called as the maxillary arch Horizontal

projection is the palatine process forming the anterior three-quarter of the hard palates. Opening of maxilla, inferior to the orbit is the infraorbital foramen which acts as a passage for blood vessels, and nerves.

- **Two zygomatic bones :** These are also called as cheek bones. They form the prominences of the cheeks, floor of the orbit and part of the lateral wall. They articulate with temporal, frontal, zygomatic and sphenoid bones.

- **Mandible :** Mandible is the largest and strongest bone of the face and is the only movable bone of the skull and it is also known as lower jaw. It consists of a curved body on the superior surface consisting of teeth and two perpendicular portions known as rami. Each ramus (plural-rami) has posterior condylar process which articulates with temporal bone and forms the temperomandibular joint and anterior coronoid process which articulates to muscles and ligaments. The point at which ramus joins the body is called as the angle of jaw.

- **Two lacrimal bones :** These are thin, nail shaped and are the smallest bones of the face. These bones are posterior and lateral to the nasal bones, form the part of wall of each orbit. Each bone has a vertical tunnel called lacrimal fossa and accommodate lacrimal sac.

- **Two palatine bones :** They are L-shaped, form the part of floor and lateral wall of the nasal cavity, posterior to hard palate and floor of the orbit.

- **Two inferior nasal conchae :** These scroll like bones form a part of inferior lateral wall of nasal cavity and project into nasal cavity. Nasal conchae increase the nasal surface area and help swirl and filter the air before its entry into the lungs.

- **Vomer :** The vomer is a triangular bone that attaches superiorly to ethmoid and sphenoid bones and inferior to maxillae and palatine bones. It divides the two nasal cavities into the right and left side.

Hyoid bone : It is a unique bone of the axial skeleton; it does not articulate with any other bone. It is located anterior to neck and below the mandible. It supports tongue and thus provides attachment site for muscles of tongue, neck and pharynx.

EXERCISE

1. Enlist the various bones of the skull.
2. What is skull? Give the types of bones of the skull.
3. Enlist and discuss the cranial and facial bones.
4. Give the names of facial bones.
5. Write a note on hyoid bone.

EXPERIMENT NO. 29

STUDY OF THE PECTORAL GIRDLE AND BONES OF THE UPPER LIMB

➢ Aim

To study the human pectoral girdle and bones of the upper limb

➢ Theory

Pectoral Girdle:

The pectoral girdle or shoulder attaches the bones of the upper limbs to the skeleton. There are two pectoral girdles consisting of clavicle and scapula.

Clavicle : It is an 'S' shaped bone, also known as collar bone. It is positioned horizontally across the frontal part of the thorax, superior to the first rib (figure 29.1). It has convex and concave curves, and the junction between these form the delicate region of the clavicle most likely to fracture. It articulates with manubrium of the sternum and forms the sternoclavicular joint. Clavicle articulates with scapula at acrominoclavicular joint and with humerus at the shoulder joint. The clavicle transmits force from the upper limb to axial skeleton and also provides attachments for the muscles.

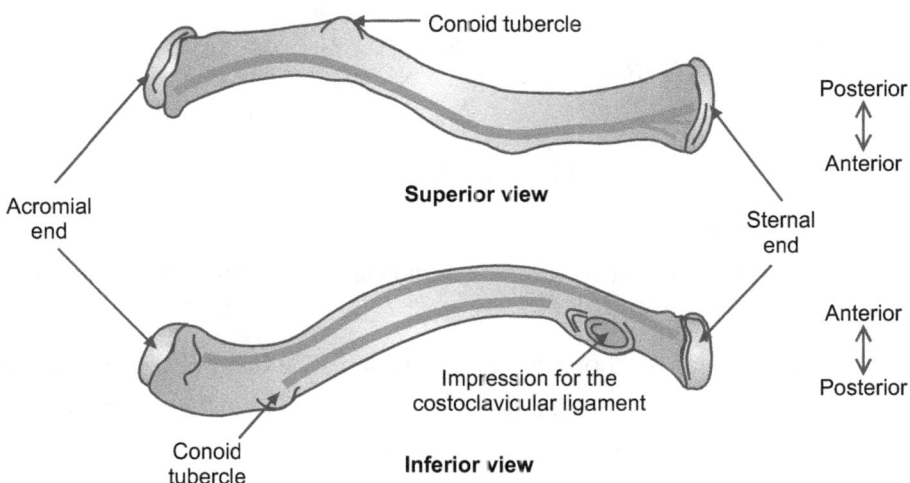

Figure 29.1 : Clavicle bone or Collar bone

Scapula (shoulder blade) : It is flat and triangular shaped, located on the back surface of the chest wall and is superficial to the ribs (figure 29.2). From the lateral side, it has shallow surface known as glenoid cavity which is involved in the formation of shoulder joint with the head of the humerus. Spine is a rough ridge on the posterior part of the body, which extends beyond the lateral border of the scapula and overhangs the glenoid cavity. The acromion process with clavicle forms the joint called as acrominoclavicular joint, a slightly movable synovial joint responsible for the movement of shoulder girdle. The coracoid process, is a projection from upper boarder portion of the scapula that provides attachment to muscle and gives movements to shoulder joint.

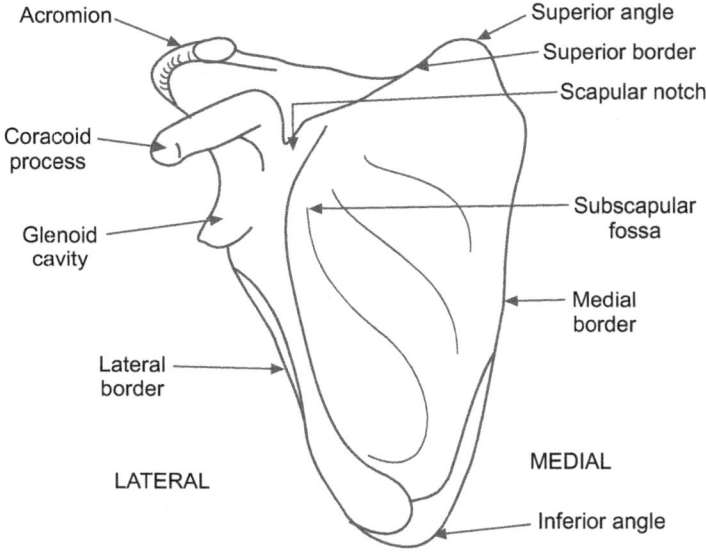

Figure 29.2: Scapula

Bones of the upper limb

Bones of upper limb consist of humerus, radius and ulna, wrist bones, bones of hand, finger bones etc.

Humerus : It is the longest bone of the upper limb. The head of the humerus fits into the glenoid cavity of scapula, forming the shoulder joint also called as socket joint. The greater and lesser tubercles are the two rough projections of humerus. There is a deep groove present between these two tubercles known as bicipital groove (figure 29.3). The distal end of the humerus presents two surfaces that articulate with the radius and ulna to form the elbow joint.

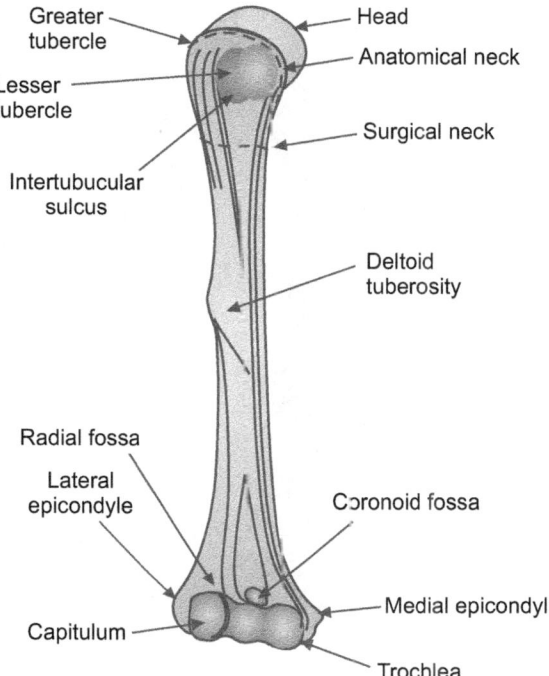

Figure 29.3: Humerus

Radius and ulna : The radius is the smaller bone and situated on the lateral side of the forearm. Its proximal end is narrow, having disc shaped head which articulates with capitulum of the humerus and the radial notch of the ulna, where as the distal end is wider (figure 29.4). Adjacent to the head of the radius is the neck, and roughened area inferior to neck is the radial tuberosity, which is a point of attachment of tendons of biceps muscle. At the distal part of the radius, there is wider shaft forming a styloid process on the lateral side which gives attachment to brachioradialis muscle and radial collateral ligament to wrist part of the hand.

The ulna is located on the medial part of the forearm and is larger than the radius. The olecranon, the proximal end, forms the prominence of the elbow. An anterior projection to the olecranon is the coronoid process which attaches with trochlea of the humerus. The distal end of the ulna consists of head which is separated from the wrist by disc of fibrocartilage. Posterior to ulna's distal end there is styloid process, which gives attachment for the ulnar collateral ligament to the wrist. Both the radius and ulna form the elbow joint with the humerus.

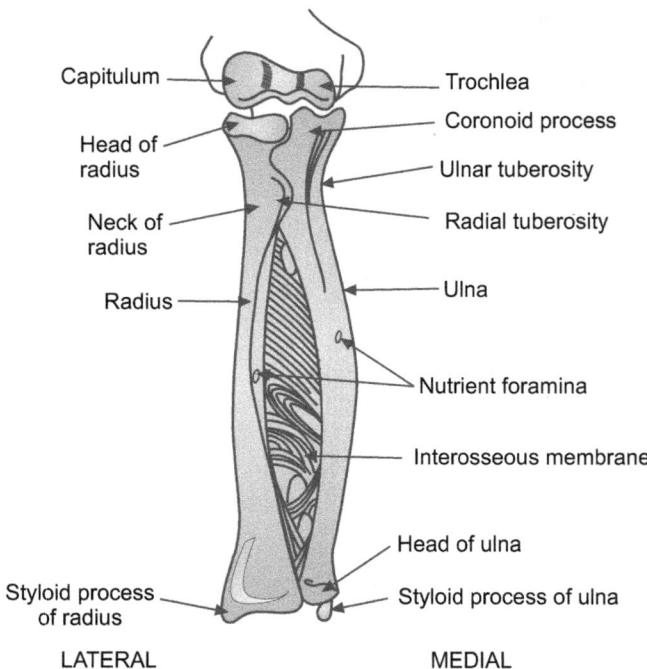

Figure 29.4: Radius and ulna

Wrist (carpal) bones : The eight carpal bones, closely fitted and arranged into two rows i.e. proximal (scaphoid, lunate, triquetrum, pisiform) and distal rows (trapezium, trapezoid, capitates, hamate). The proximal bones of carpal are associated with the writ joint whereas distal bones form the joints with metacarpal bones.

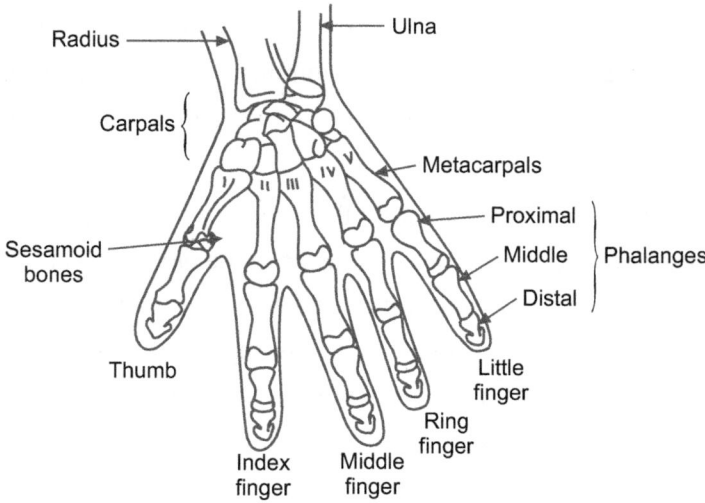

Figure 29.5 : Carpal, metacarpal and phalanges

Metacarpal bones : The fives bones of the palm of the hand are called as metacarpal bones. The proximal ends articulate with carpal bones and distal ends with phalanges.

Phalanges : There are 14 phalanges, 3 in each finger, and 2 in thumb. Phalanges articulate to metacarpal bone and with each other by hinge joint (figure 29.5).

> **Thoracic cage**

Thoracic cage consists of bones of a sternum, 12 pairs of ribs and 12 thoracic vertebrae

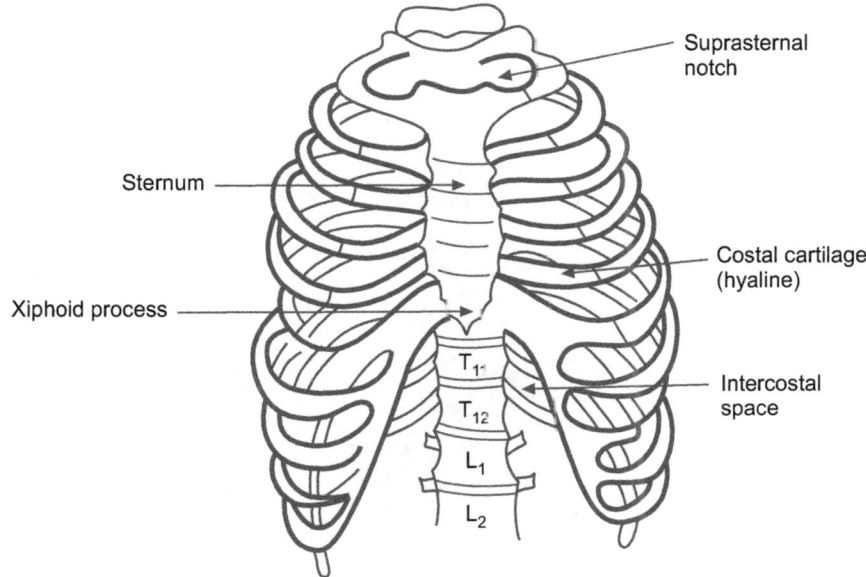

Figure 29.6: Thoracic cage

Sternum : It is also known as breastbone. It is flat, narrow, 'T' shaped, lies in the middle of the anterior thoracic wall and has 3 parts; manubrium, gladiolus and xiphoid process (figure 29.6). It connects to the rib bones through cartilage, forming the anterior section of the rib cage with them, and thus helps to protect the lungs, heart and from physical trauma.

EXERCISE

1. Enlist the bones of the pectoral girdle.
2. Name the joints when clavicle articulates with other bones of the upper limb.
3. Enlist the bones of the upper limb.
4. Give in brief the role of clavicle, scapula, ribs, humerus, and radius ulna.

❖ ❖ ❖

EXPERIMENT NO. 30

STUDY OF BONES OF THE VERTEBRAL COLUMN

➢ Aim

To study the bones of the vertebral column

➢ Theory

The vertebral column is known as backbone or spinal column and with the thoracic cage it forms the skeleton of the trunk of the body. The major functions of the vertebral column are to facilitate the forward, backward and sideways movements. It serves as a point of attachment to the thoracic cage and muscle, protects the spinal cord and provides support to the head.

There are a total 26 vertebrae which include 7 cervical vertebrae at the neck region; 12 thoracic vertebrae posterior to thoracic cavity; 5 lumbar, 1 sacrum and 1 coccyx. The sacrum and coccyx are the immovable bones while others are movable.

➢ Cervical vertebrae

A total of 7 cervical vertebrae smaller than thoracic vertebrae make up 3 foramina i.e. 2 transverse and 1 vertebral foramina having vein and nerve fibers passing through.

Atlas : It is the first and topmost cervical vertebra, and along with the axis, it forms the joint connecting the skull and spine. Atlas is a large ring like structure without body, consisting of an anterior and a posterior arch and two lateral masses.

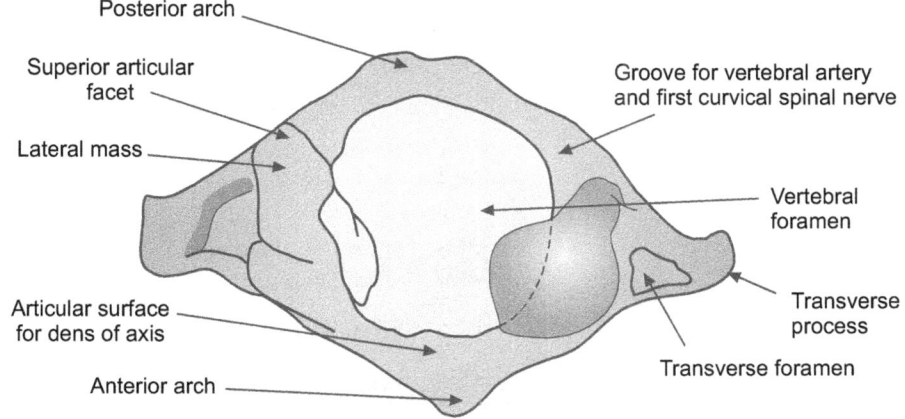

Figure 30.1: Atlas Vertebra

The superior articular facets of atlas articulate with occipital condyles of the occipital bone (figure 30.1) to form the atlanto-occipital joint which gives the 'YES' saying movement (up and down movements) of skull. The inferior articular facets articulate with axis.

Axis : It is the second cervical vertebra, and has a strong odontoid process which rises perpendicularly from the upper surface of the body (figure 30.2). It forms the pivot joint by articulating with atlas which helps during the rotating of head side to side.

The other 4 cervical vertebrae consist of bifid spinous processes and 7th is non bifid spinous and serve as essential anatomical landmark.

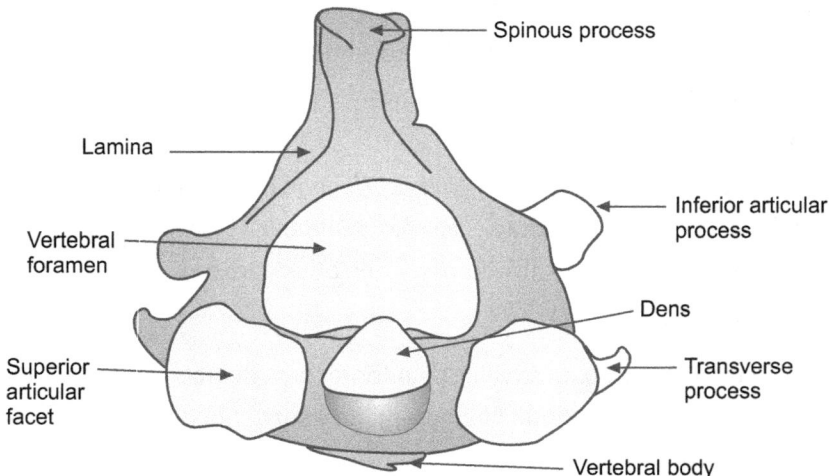

Figure 30.2 : Axis

> **Thoracic vertebrae**

Thoracic vertebrae are 12 in numbers which are larger and stronger than other vertebrae. It articulates with ribs to form facets (figure 30.3).

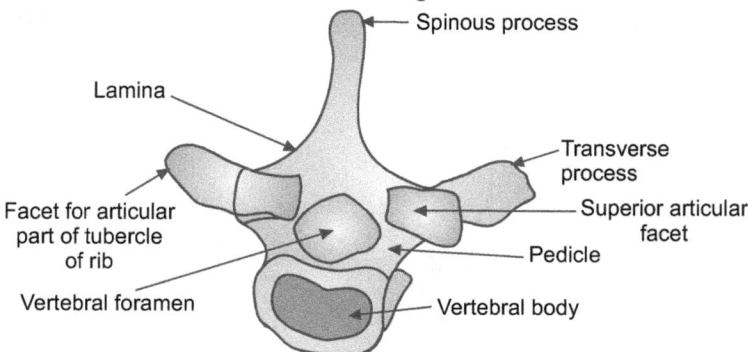

Figure 30.3 : Thoracic vertebra

It consists of heart shaped body, downward pointed spinous processes, two facets present, on either side, two costal semi-facets, one above, near the root of the pedicle, the other below in front of the inferior vertebral notch. A small facet at the tips of the transverse process articulates with tubercles of the ribs.

> **The lumber vertebrae**

They are 5 in number and is the largest vertebrae of the column. The body is kidney shaped and does not articulate with ribs (figure 30.4). The spinous processes of this vertebra are flat and stout and have backward projection and provide attachment for the back muscles.

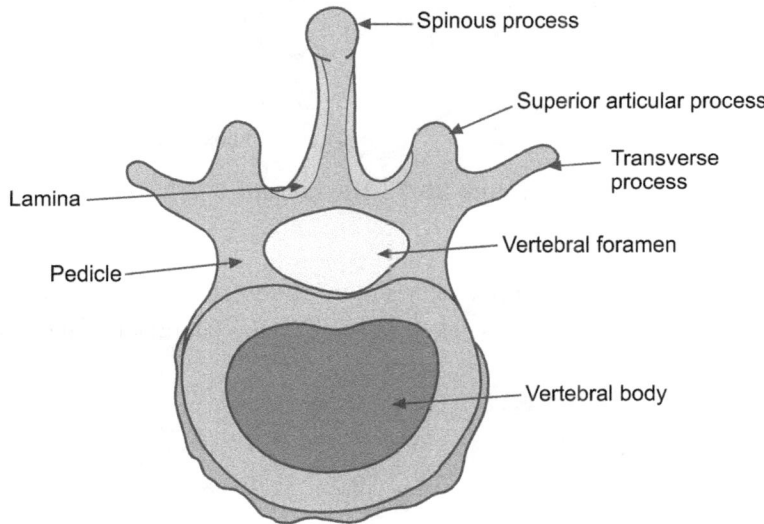

Figure 30.4 : Lumbar vertebra

> **The sacrum**

The sacrum is a triangular bone formed by the collection of five sacral vertebrae which articulates to the 5th lumbar vertebrae and forms the lumbo-sacral angle and below with the coccyx (figure 30.5). The body is large and much wider from side to side than from backwards. Its anterior projecting edge is named the sacral promontory. Transverse process and the costal element are fused to each other to form the upper surface of the lateral mass of the sacrum on both sides. Its base projects forward and upward forming the prominent sacrovertebral angle when articulated with the last lumbar vertebra. Its central part is projected backward, so as to give increased capacity to the pelvic cavity. In between the body and lateral masses contain anterior sacral foramina which offer gap for passage of nerves. The inferior surface of the sacrum articulates with coccyx.

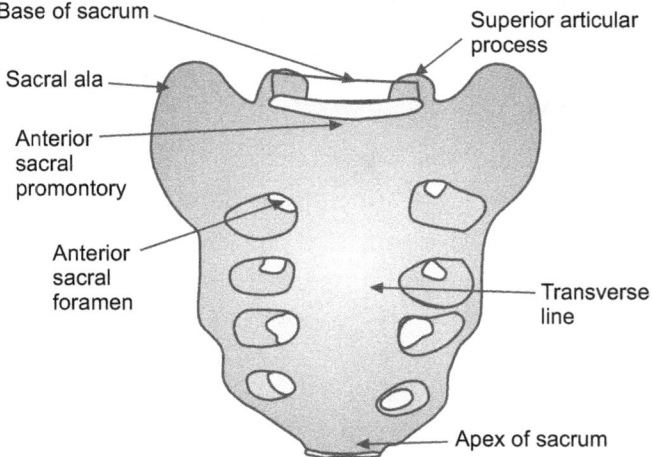

Figure 30.5 : The sacrum

> **The coccyx**

It is triangular, single, fused with 4 rudimentary vertebrae. Superiorly, it articulates with sacrum and contains a series of transverse processes on the lateral surface (figure 30.6).

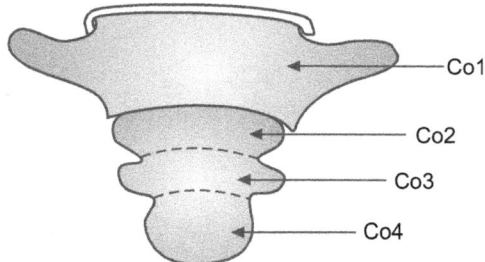

Figure 30.6 : The coccyx

EXERCISE

1. Enlist the bones of the vertebral column
2. Give the locations of the thoracic vertebrae.
3. What are the functions of the cervical vertebrae?
4. Give the total number of vertebral bones.
5. What is coccyx?

❖❖❖

EXPERIMENT NO. 31

STUDY OF THE PELVIC GIRDLE AND THE LOWER LIMB

> ## Aim

To study the human pelvic girdle and the lower limb

The pelvic girdle :The two hip bones, i.e. sacrum and coccyx form the basin shaped structure known as pelvic girdle.

The hip bones : The hip bone consists of three fused bones, mainly ilium, ischium and pubis. On the lateral side of the hip bone there is a depression known as acetabulum, responsible for formation of hip joint with the femur. The ilium, the upper flattened part of the hip bone presents the iliac crest, an anterior curve of which is known as anterior superior iliac spine (figure 31.1). The synovial joint is formed by ilium with the sacrum, and it helps in the absorption of stress due to weight. The ischium forms the inferior and back part of the hip bone that lies below the ilium and behind the pubis and is the strongest part of the three bones that forms the hip bone. The tuberosity of the ischium is a large swelling which bears the body's weight during seating posture. The last bone i.e. pubis forms the anterior part and forms the cartilaginous joint by articulating with symphysis pubis.

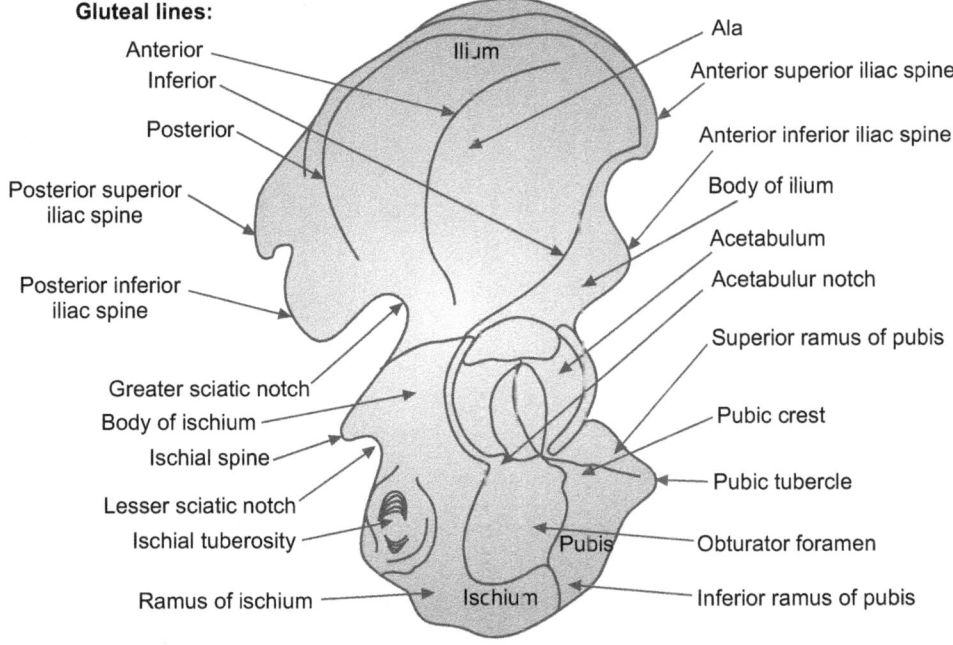

Figure 31.1: Hip bone

➤ Bones of the lower limb

Bones of the lower limb includes femur, tibia, fibula, patella, tarsal bones, metatarsals, and phalanges

Femur : It is also known as thigh bone and is the strongest, heaviest and longest bone of the body (figure 31.2). The proximal end of the femur is the head which forms the hip joint with acetabulum of the hip bone. The head region contains depression known as fovea capitis which attaches with the acetabulum through ligaments. The distal end of the femur is constricted and is known as neck. At the junctions of the neck emerge two projections, greater trochanter and lesser trochanter which provide points of attachment for the tendons of thigh and buttock muscles. The greater tronchanter is used to locate the site for intramuscular injections into the thigh. The intertrochanteric crest is a bony ridge found on the posterior surface of the tronchanter, gluteal tuberosity and linea aspera (ridge of roughened surface on the posterior aspect of the femur. These ridges provide attachment points for the tendons of various thigh muscles. The distal end of the femur contains medial and lateral condyle. Superior to this condyle is the epicondyle, to which ligaments of the knee joints attach. The function of the femur is to transmit the weight of the body to the bones below the knee.

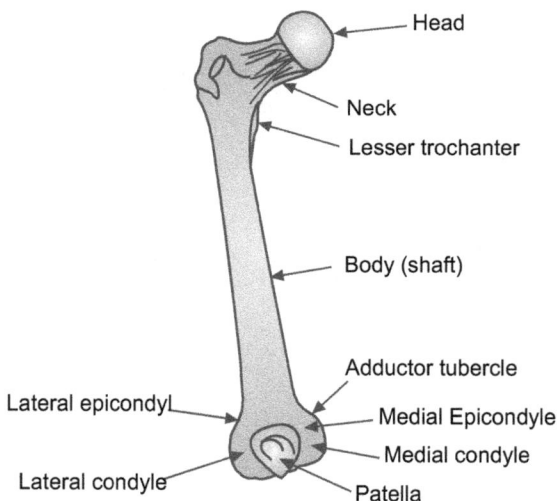

Figure 31.2: Femur

Tibia : It is the larger and stronger of the two bones of the lower limbs. The proximal extremity is broad and flat and presents two condyles that articulate with femur at knee joint. The head of tibia articulates inferior to the lateral condyle, forming the proximal tibiofibular joint (figure 31.3).

Fibula : It is smaller and parallel to the tibia and does not articulate with femur but supports the stabilisation of the ankle joint. It forms the proximal tibiofibular joint when its head articulates with the inferior surface of the lateral condyle of the tibia below the knee joint (figure 31.3).

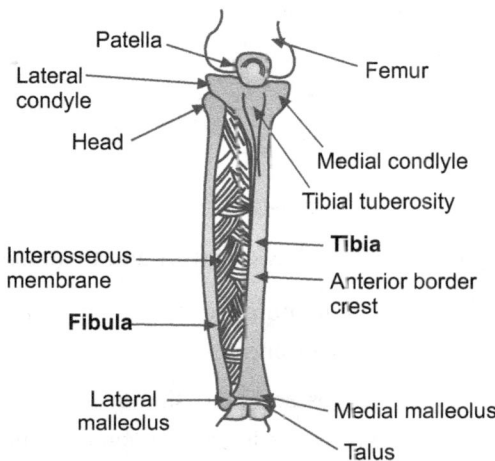

Figure 31.3 : Tibia and Fibula

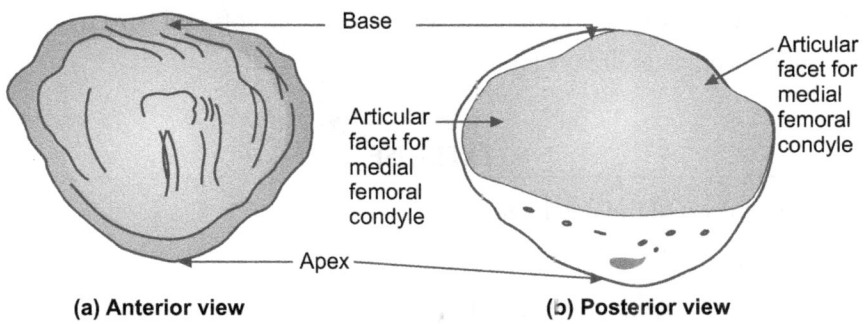

Figure 31.4 : Patella

Patella : It is a triangular, sesamoid bone associated with the knee joint, which positioned with the apex projecting downwards. Its anterior surface is in the patellar tendon and the posterior surface articulates with patellar surface of the femur in the knee joint (figures 31.4).

Tarsal bones : The seven tarsal bones forms the posterior part of the foot, which includes, talus-articulates with tibia and fibula at the knee joint, calcaneus-provides attachments for muscles, navicular, cuboid and three cuneiform-articulate with each other and with metatarsal bones (figure 31.5).

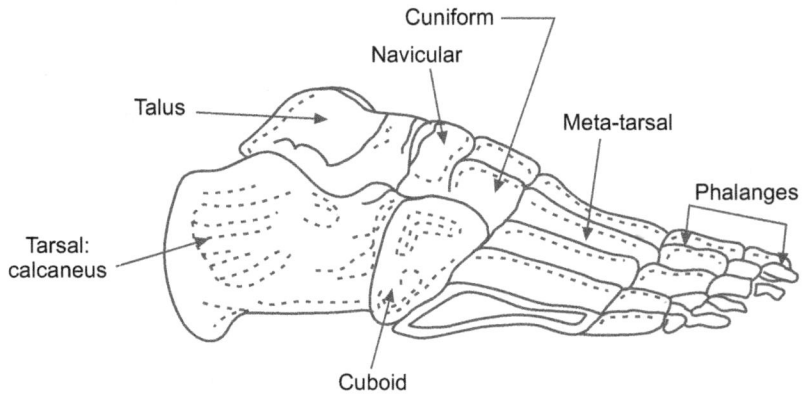

Figure 31.5: Tarsal, Metatarsal and Phalanges

Metatarsal bones : These are 5 in number; form the greater part of the foot. The proximal end articulates with tarsal bones and the distal end with phalanges (figure 31.5).

Phalanges : There are 14 phalanges arranged similar to that of the fingers. The joints between phalanges of the foot are known as interphalangeal joints(figure 31.5).

The arrangements of the bones of foot are associated with ligaments and muscles, which give the sole of the foot an arched or curved shape. The arches i.e. longitudinal and transverse enable ideal distribution of body weight over the soft and hard tissue of the foot and also provide leverage while walking.

EXERCISE

1. Name the bones of the pelvic girdle.
2. Enlist the various bones of the lower limb.
3. Give the role of femur, tibia and fibula

EXPERIMENT NO. 32

STUDY OF VARIOUS JOINTS

➤ Aim

To study the various human joints

➤ Theory

Joint is a point of attachment or contact between two bones or between bones and cartilages, or teeth. Joint is also called as articulation.

Joints are classified into

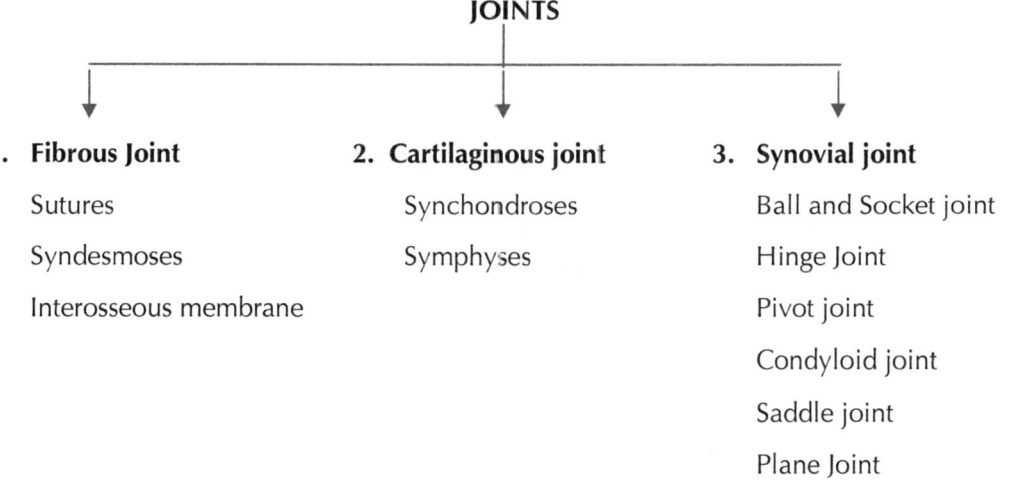

1. Fibrous Joint	2. Cartilaginous joint	3. Synovial joint
Sutures	Synchondroses	Ball and Socket joint
Syndesmoses	Symphyses	Hinge Joint
Interosseous membrane		Pivot joint
		Condyloid joint
		Saddle joint
		Plane Joint

1. Fibrous joints

Fibrous joint holds the other articulating bones closely together by dense irregular connective tissue and is without synovial cavity; thus these joints do not move or show little movements.

Sutures : It consists of thin irregular connective tissue that join the bones of the skull together by its interlocking edges (figure 32.1). The interlocking edges offer strength, and reduces chances of fracture and also acts as shock absorbent.

Syndesmoses : These are fibrous joints, articulate two bones and are arranged as ligaments which permit limited movements of bones (figure 32.2).

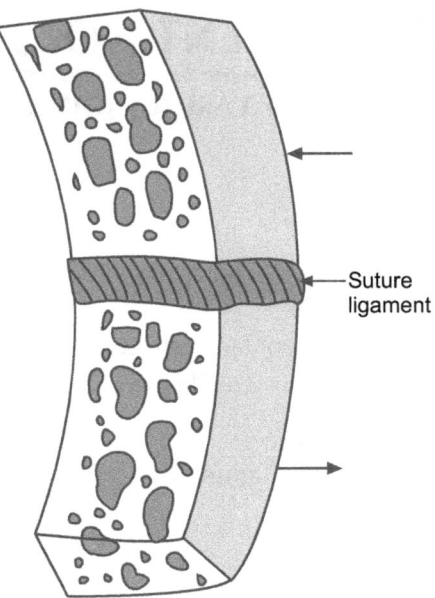

Figure 32.1 : Suture ligaments

Interosseous membrane : It consists of dense irregular connective tissue which binds the adjacent bone and allows slight movements e.g. interosseous membrane between radius and ulna; tibia and fibula (figure 32.3).

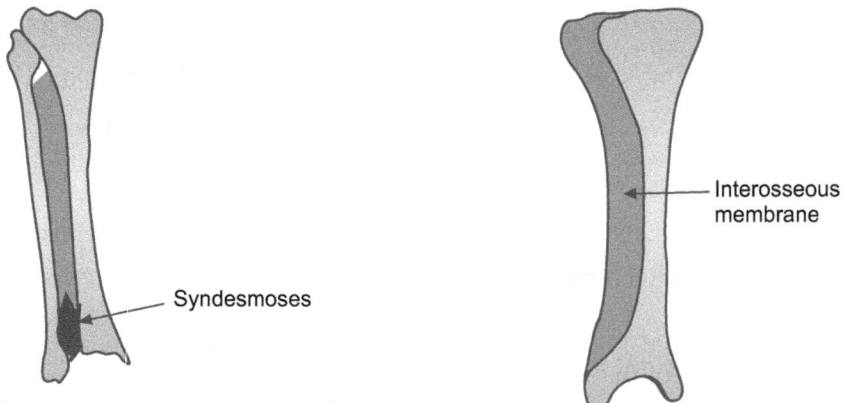

Figure 32.2 : Syndesmoses of tibia and fibula

Figure 32.3 : Interosseous membrane between tibia and fibula

2. Cartilaginous joints

Cartilaginous joints permit slow movements or no movements due to absence of synovial cavity. The bones of these joints are tightly joined by hyaline cartilages.

Synchondroses : It is a cartilaginous joint in which the epipyseal plate of each end of a long bone connects the epiphysis of growing bones by either hyaline cartilage or fibrocartilage (figure 32.4).

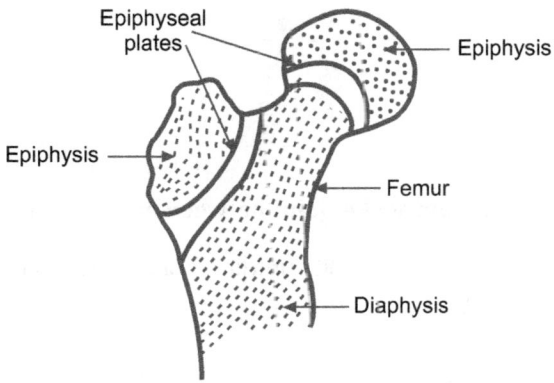

Figure 32.4 : Synchondrosis

Symphyses : The ends of articulating bones are covered with hyaline cartilage and connect the bones. e.g. the pubic symphyses found in symphysis between the frontal surfaces of hip bone (figure 32.5).

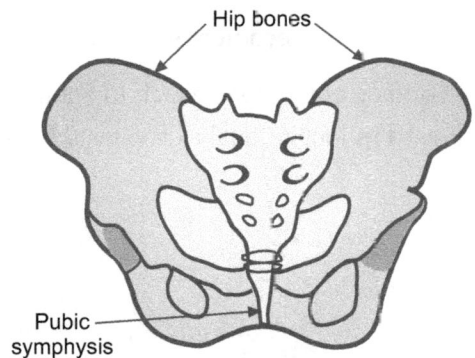

Figure 32.5: Symphysis

3. **Synovial joints**

It consists of synovial cavity which offers movements of joints and thus these joints are freely movable. The cartilages of these joints are smooth and slippery for free movements.

Ball and socket joint : It consist of depression or cavity on one side of a bone and ball like surface on the another bone, this arrangements permits them to fit closely to each other and allows free movements. The shoulder and hip joints are the examples of ball and socket joint (figure 32.6).

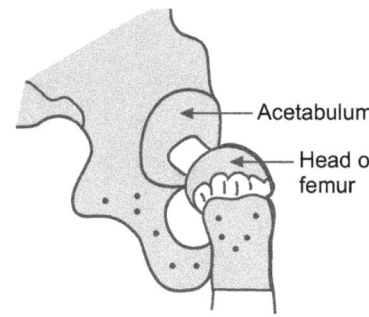

Figure 32.6: Ball and socket joint between acetabulum and femur

Hinge joints : These joints permit unidirectional movements e.g. elbow joint, interphalangeal joint (figure 32.7).

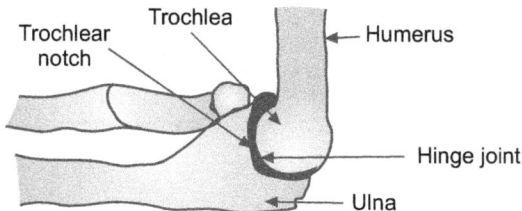

Figure 32.7 : Hinge joint between humerus and ulna (at elbow joint)

Pivot joints : The round surface of the bone attach to another bone partly by ligaments and allow the movement around its longitudinal axis. e.g. atlanto-axial joint (figure 32.8)

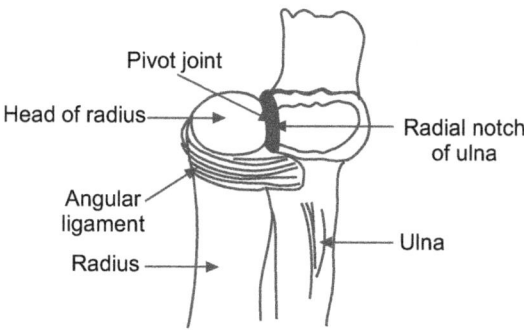

Figure 32 .8 : Pivot joint between head and radius and radial notch of ulna

Condyloid joints or ellipsoidal joints : It is the convex oval shaped bone fused into depression of another bone and permits two sided movements e.g. radiocarpal and metacarpophalangeal joints (figure 32.9).

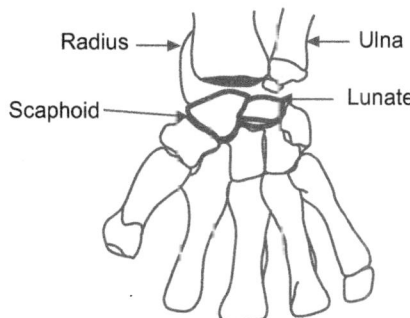

Figure 32.9: Condyloid joint of radius and lunate and scaphoid bones of carpus (wrist joint)

Saddle joint or seller joint : In this, one bone is saddle shaped and the other bone is fused into the saddle. It allows the two sides movements same as that of ellipsoidal joints. e.g. carpometacarpal joints (figure 32.10).

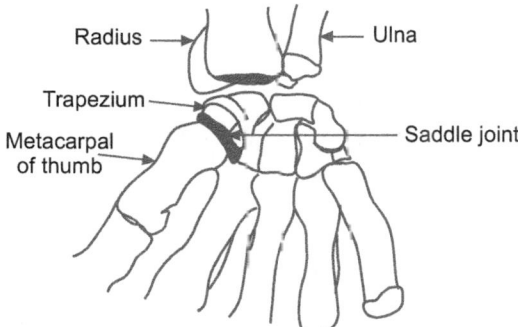

Figure 32.10 : Saddle joint between trupezium of capus and metacarpal of thumb

> **Significance**

Rheumatism : It is the disorder of joints and connective tissues characterised by pain, inflammation and difficulty to initiate movements.

Osteoarthritis : It is a group of mechanical abnormalities involving degradation of joints, including articular cartilage and subchondral bone characterised by pain, tenderness, stiffness, and locking.

Rheumatoid arthritis : It is an autoimmune disease that results in a chronic, systemic inflammatory disorder that may affect many tissues and organs. It is characterised by inflammation of joints, swelling and loss of function.

Ankylosing spondylitis is a chronic inflammatory disease of the axial skeleton with variable involvement of peripheral joints and nonarticular structures. It is characterised by pain and stiffness in the hips and lower back that progress upward along the backbone.

EXERCISE

1. Define a joint. Give the classification of joints with examples
2. What are fibrous joints? Enlist joints of the fibrous types.
3. Enlist the synovial joints.
4. Why are the fibrous and cartilaginous joints immovable?
5. Explain the following terminology
   (a) Rheumatism
   (b) Osteoarthritis
   (c) Rheumatoid arthritis
   (d) Ankylosing spondylitis

EXPERIMENT NO. 33

STUDY OF THE CENTRAL NERVOUS SYSTEM

➢ **Aim**

To study the human central nervous system (CNS)

➢ **Theory**

Nervous system is divided into -

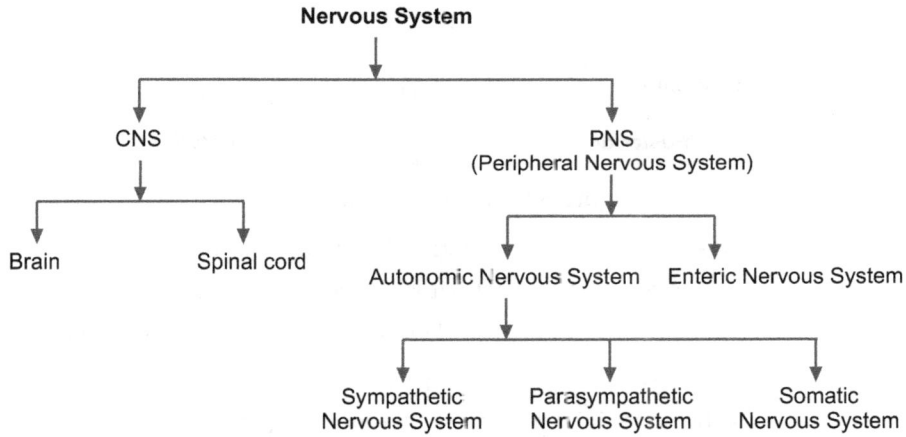

The CNS : The main function of CNS is to maintain integration of sensory input and motor output, thus it enables a person to identify sensory information and formulate responses to changes that alter haemostatic balance. Apart from this function, the nervous system is also involved in perceptions, behaviours, memories, and all voluntary movements. The nerves (neurons) are a bundle of thousands of axons plus associated connective tissue and blood vessels that lie outside the brain and spinal cord.

The CNS consists of brain and spinal cord

The Brain : The brain lies within the cranial cavity, and constitutes $1/5^{th}$ of the body weight and consists of cerebrum, brain stem (mid brain, pons), medulla oblongata, and cerebellum (figure 33.1).

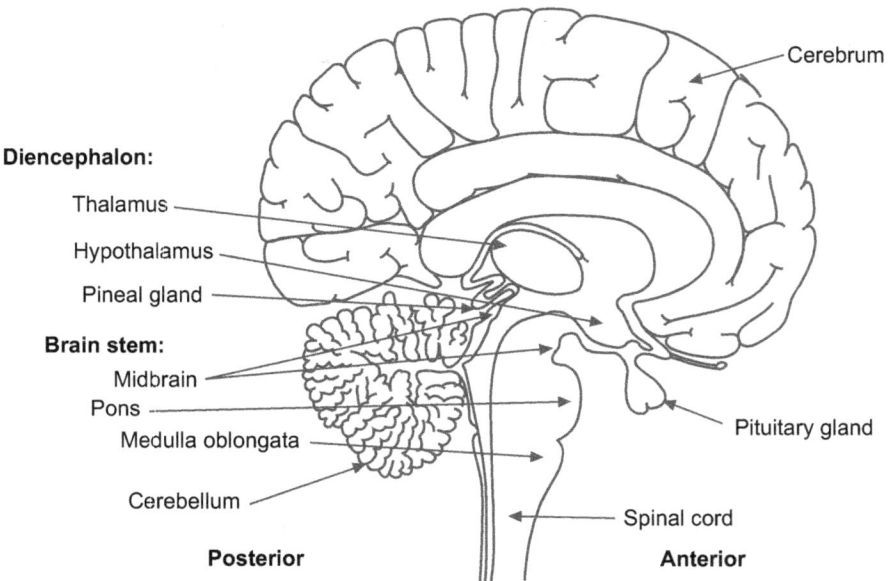

Figure 33.1 : The Human Brain

Cerebrum : It is the seat of intelligence and is the largest part of the brain and occupies anterior and middle part of the cranial cavity. It is derived by a deep cleft into right and left cerebral hemispheres. Inside the brain, the two hemispheres are connected by corpus callosum.

Cerebral cortex is the superficial part of the cerebrum. Hemisphere of cerebrum has 4 lobes viz; frontal, parietal, temporal and occipital lobes.

Function of cerebrum : Mental activities are involved in memory, intelligence, sense of responsibility, thinking, reasoning, moral sense and learning.

- Sensory perception (pain, temperature, tough, taste, smell)
- Initiation and control of voluntary muscle contraction

Functional areas of cerebrum

1. Motor area
2. Sensory area
3. Brain Stem

(b) Mid brain : It is situated around the cerebral aqueduct between the cerebrum above and pons varolii below. It connects the cerebrum with lower parts of the brain and spinal cord.

(c) Pons varolii : It is situated in front of the cerebellum, below the mid brain and above the medulla oblongata. It consists of nerve fibers forming a bridge between the two hemispheres of cerebellum and of fibers passing between the higher level of brain and the spinal cord.

(d) Medulla oblongata : Extends from the pons varolii above and is continuous with the spinal cord below. It is pyramid shaped and it lies within the cranium above the foramen magnum .Its anterior and posterior surfaces are marked by central fissures. Cells of the medulla oblongata consist of relay stations for sensory nerves passing from spinal cord to cerebrum.

Vital centers present in medulla oblongata are given as below.

1. Cardiac centre – controls functioning of the heart.
2. Respiratory centre – controls rate and depth of respiration.
3. Vasomotor centre – controls the diameter of blood vessels.
4. Reflex centre – for vomiting, coughing, sneezing, swallowing.

Decussation of pyramids : Motor nerves descending from the motor area in the cerebrum to the spinal cord in the pyramidal or cortico spinal tract, crossing from left side to the right and vice versa in the medulla oblongata.

2. Cerebellum : The second largest part of the brain, situated posterior to pons varolii and immediately below the posterior portion of the cerebrum lying posterior to cranial fossa. It has two hemispheres, separated by narrow median strip called as gray matter which is found on the surface, while white matter is present inside the cerebellum.

Cerebellum performs functions like coordination of voluntary movement, posture, balance and coordinates activities associated with maintenance of balance and equilibrium of the body.

➢ Spinal cord

It is elongated and almost cylindrical part extending from the brain just below the medulla. It is suspended in the vertebral canal and is surrounded by three meninges and cerebrospinal fluid

Meninges are : 1) dura matter, 2) arachnoids and 3) pia matter.

The spinal cord extends from the first cervical vertebra to the lower border of the first lumber vertebrae, is approximately 42-45 cm long and is about the thickness of the little finger (figure 33.2).

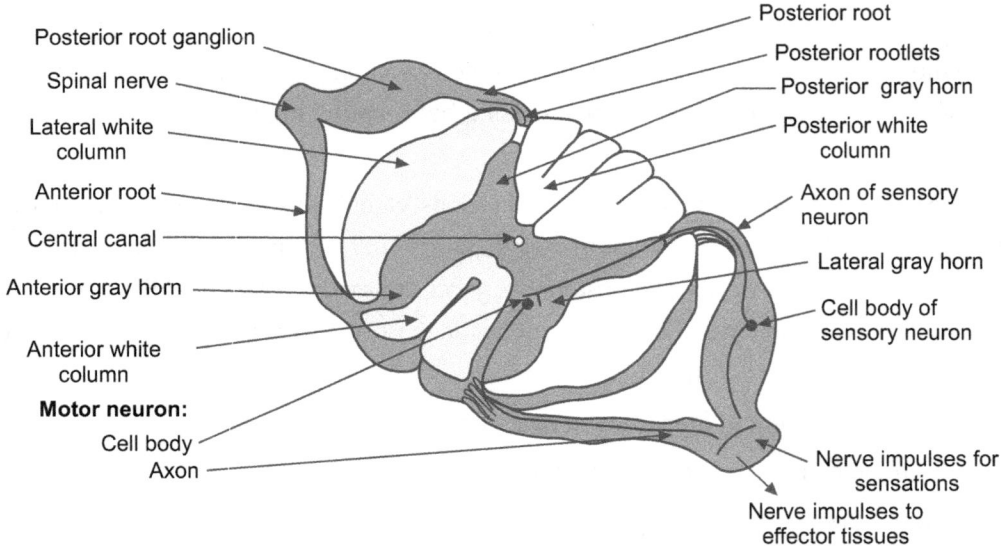

Figure 33.2 : Spinal cord

The spinal cord is the nervous tissue link between the brain and the rest of the body, except the cranial nerves. Motor nerves originating from the brain descend through the spinal cord and supply to various organs and tissues at the appropriate level of the cord. Sensory nerves from different organs and tissue enter and pass through the spinal cord to the brain. This sensory information is conveyed by the dorsal nerve route and spinal cord. The cell bodies of these unipolar, sensory neurons make up a small region of gray matter in the dorsal root ganglia; while fibers of the ventral nerve root carry motor information out of the spinal cord. Cell bodies of these multipolar, motor neurons are in grey motor area that composes the inner core of the spinal cord.

Diencephelon – extends from the brain stem to the cerebrum and surrounds the third ventricle.

It comprises of the thalamus, hypothalamus and epithalamus.

The thalamus has important structures, which relay sensory impulses from the sensory areas to the spinal cord and brain stem. The thalamus receives, relays, and transmits sensory and motor information to and from the cerebral cortex.

Inferiorly to the thalamus is the hypothalamus having a number of nuclei; those involved in various behavioral and physiological functions.

> **Important functions of the hypothalamus are given below**

Regulation of ANS functions like contraction of smooth muscle and cardiac muscle; production of hormones, regulation of emotions and behaviour, food and water intake, equilibrium, control of body temperature and circulating circadian symptoms and consciousness.

Epithalmus is superior to thalamus and contains pineal gland which secretes melatonin involved in induction of sleepiness.

The arrangement of grey matter in the spinal cord resembles the shape of the letter H, having two posterior, two anterior and two lateral columns. The area of grey matter lying transversely is the transverse commissure and it is pierced by the central canal, an extension from the fourth ventricle, containing cerebrospinal fluid.

The white matter of the spinal cord is arranged in three columns or tracts; anterior, posterior and lateral. These tracts are formed by sensory nerve fibers ascending to the brain, motor nerve fibers descending from the brain and fibers of connector neurons.

There are two main sources of sensation transmitted to the brain via the spinal cord.

1. The skin : Sensory receptors (nerve endings) in the skin, called cutaneous receptors, are stimulated by pain, heat, cold and touch, including pressure. Nerve impulses generated are conducted by three neurons to the sensory area in the opposite hemisphere of the cerebrum where the sensation and its location are perceived.

2. The tendons, muscles and joints : Sensory receptors are nerve endings in these structures, called proprioceptors, which are activated in response to stretch phenomenon. Together with impulses from the eyes and the ears they are associated with the maintenance of balance and posture and with perception of the position of the body in space.

Motor neuron stimulation results in contraction of skeletal (striated, voluntary) muscle, contraction of smooth (involuntary) muscle, cardiac muscle and the secretion by glands controlled by nerves of the autonomic nervous system.

> **Spinal Cord Physiology**

It provides conduction pathways to and from the brain and serves as the integrator or reflex center for all spinal reflexes. The white matter tracts in the spinal cord are highways for nerve impulse propagation. The grey matter of the spinal cord receives and integrates incoming and outgoing information.

➢ Pathological Significance

Stroke : It is a neurological disorder due to blockade of blood vessels which supply blood to the brain tissue. Symptoms include paralysis of one part of the body (hemiplegia), loss of sensation, slurred speech, death may also occur.

Predisposing factors include hypertension, atheroma, cigarette smoking, diabetes mellitus, blood clot, high cholesterol in blood vessels, stress etc.

Dementia : It is a permanent or progressive loss of intellectual abilities i.e. impairment of memory, judgment, obstruct twinkling etc.

Meningitis : Inflammation of meninges due to infection caused by bacteria or virus. Symptoms include fever, headache, vomiting, confusion, lethargy and drowsiness.

Epilepsy : It is the disorder of CNS characterised by periodical and unpredictable occurrence of seizures. Seizures occur because of rhythmic, synchronic discharge of neurons due to hyper activity leading to behaviour impairment with or without affecting the motor activity. Depending upon the factors and part of the brain involved, it is of two types, generalised (throughout brain) and partial (local).

Various antiepileptic drugs used in the treatment include- Benzodiazepines, barbiturates, valproic acid, phenytoin etc. alone in combination for certain period.

Depression : Depression is a feeling of intense sadness or unhappiness. It develops due to illness, hormonal imbalance, environmental factors, genetics etc.

Management of depression can be done by psychotherapy and drug treatment (imipramine, fluoxetine etc).

EXERCISE

1. Give the main functions of the CNS.
2. Enlist the various structural parts of the brain.
3. Give the functions of hypothalamus.
4. Give the physiology of spinal cord.
5. Define the following term
   (a) Depression
   (b) Dementia
   (c) Meningitis
   (d) Epilepsy

EXPERIMENT NO. 34

STUDY OF THE LYMPHATIC SYSTEM

➢ Aim

To study the lymphatic system

➢ Theory

The lymphatic system is a part of the circulatory system consisting of a network of, lymphatic vessels for transportation of lymph. Lymphatic tissue is a reticular connective tissue that contains a large number of B and T cells (lymphocytes). Lymph enters via vessels of increasing size into a large number of lymph nodes before returning to blood circulation. The lymphatic system helps in circulating body fluids and in defense against diseases causing agents

➢ Lymph and lymph capillaries

Lymph is a clear, pale yellow fluid (in intestine it is creamy white), similar in composition to that of plasma and interstitial fluid and varies in plasma protein content. It transports the lymphocytes, plasma proteins, bacteria and cell debris of damaged tissues which is filtered and destroyed by lymph nodes.

Lymph capillaries are composed of a single layer of endothelial cells that originate as blind end in the interstitial space. They are more permeable to proteins and cell debris. The minute capillaries join together to form larger lymph vessels which cover the arteries and veins. Lymph vessels consist of numerous cup shaped valves that ensure the unidirectional flow of lymph towards the thorax. The contraction of adjacent muscles and regular pulsation of larger arteries induce milking action which facilitates the onward movements of lymph. The thoracic and right lymphatic ducts are formed by the association of lymph vessels together and they empty the lymph into the subclavian veins.

Lymph node : Lymph nodes are bean shaped, located along lymphatic vessels in a group. It is 1-25 mm long, covered over by a capsule of dense connective tissues that extends into the node, forming the trabeculae, which divide the node into compartments. Lymph node contains lymphocytes and macrophages. Nearly about 4-5 afferent lymph vessels enter the lymph node and only one efferent vessel carries lymph from the lymph node. Hilum is the concave surface of the lymph node, where in the artery enters and vein leaves. Internal to the capsule is a supporting network of reticular fibers and fibroblasts, which along with capsule and trabeculae constitute the stroma of the lymph node. The parenchyma of lymph node is divided into a superficial cortex and deep medulla. The superficial cortex consists of outer and inner cortex. The egg shaped B cells known as lymphatic nodules are found in outer cortex, while the inner cortex contains T cells and dendritic cells that enter the lymph node from the other tissues. The medulla contains B cells, antibody producing plasma cells and macrophages.

> **Functions of the lymph node**

1. Lymph node acts as a filter and traps foreign particles;
2. Phagocytosis i.e. engulfment of particulate matter, bacteria, cells from malignant tumor;
3. Multiplication and proliferation of T and B lymphocytes

> **Spleen**

Spleen is oval shaped, and is the largest lymphatic organ ,12 cm in length, 2.5 cm in thickness and contains reticular and lymphatic tissue (figure 34.1). It lies in the left hypochondriac region between the stomach and diaphragm. Impressions are the notches found in the adjacent organs of lymph which includes gastric impression (stomach), renal impression (left kidney), and the colic impression (left colic flexure of large intestine). Similar to lymph node, spleen also has hilum, through which splenic artery, vein and efferent lymphatic vessels enter. The capsule, trabeculae, reticular fibres and fibroblasts form the stoma; the functional part i.e. parenchyma of the spleen consists of red and white pulp. Red pulp consists of a dense network of fine reticular fibres, continuous with those of the splenic trabeculae, to which are applied flat, branching cells. The meshes of the reticulum are filled with blood. The removal of ruptured, worn out, or defective blood cells and platelets by macrophages, storage of platelets and blood cell production during foetal life are the important functions carried out in the red pulp of the spleen. The white pulp consists of lymphocytes and macrophages. The blood circulates into spleen via splenic artery as it enters the central arteries of the white pulp.

B and T cells perform immune functions and macrophages are involved in phagocytosis in white pulp of spleen.

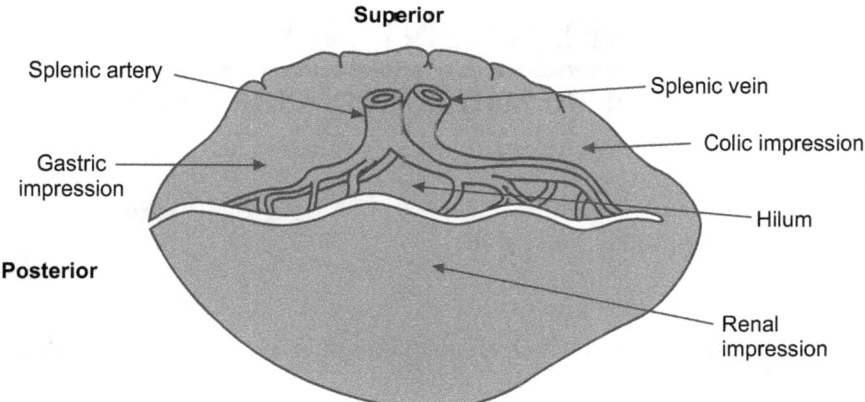

Figure 34.1 : The spleen

> **Thymus gland**

It is located anterior to the sternum and posterior to the heart having weight of approximately 30-40 g in adults. It consists of 2 lobes attached by areolar tissue. The lobules of thymus consist of framework of epithelial cells and T lymphocytes. Thymus gland is involved in development and production of mature T lymphocytes. The maturation of T lymphocytes is initiated by hormone called as 'thymosin'.

> **Pathological significance**

Lymphoma - the cancer of the lymph nodes

Hypersplenism - abnormal splenic activity because of enlargement of spleen associated with excessive destruction of blood cells.

EXERCISE

1. What is lymph?
2. Give the role of lymph capillaries.
3. What are the functions of lymph node?
4. What is spleen? Give its functions in brief.

❖❖❖

EXPERIMENT NO. 35

STUDY OF THE MALE REPRODUCTIVE SYSTEM

➢ **Aim**

To study the male reproductive system.

➢ **Theory**

Reproduction is a process in which an animal or plant produces an individual like itself.

The male reproductive system consist of external genital organs viz, scrotum, penis and urethra and internal reproductive organs such as testes, vas deferens, seminal vesicles and prostate gland bulbourethral gland etc.

Scrotum : It is a pouch like structure hanging from the base of the penis (figure 35.1). The scrotal septum divides vertically into two sacs, each one containing testes. The position of scrotum and contraction of its muscle fibers regulate the temperature of testes.

Testes : Testes are two in number, suspended in each sac of scrotum by spermatic cord. Each testis is about 5 cm in length, 2.5 cm in diameter with 10-20 gm in weight and covered by tough fibrous capsule. Each testis contains spermatogenic cells and sertoli cells in somniferous tubules, supporting the process of spermatogenesis. Somniferous tubules produce sperms, which during intercourse, enter the vagina and into fallopian tube of female reproductive system where it fertilises the ovum (released from ovaries) in the fallopian tubes. Testes are involved in spermatogenesis and secretion of male sex hormones i.e. testosterone from interstitial or Leydig cells.

Penis : It is a male genital organ for reproduction consisting of urethra for excretion of urine as well as semen ejaculation. It is cylindrical in shape and consists of glans penis, and the body. The body of the penis is composed of fibrous tissue known as tunica albugenia. The dorsolateral muscles are called the corpus cavernosa. Upon dilation of blood vessels of corpus cavernosa, erection of penis takes place causing maximum blood to enter into blood sinus (figure 35.1).

Epididymis : It is a 4 cm long, comma shaped organ that lies along the posterior border of each testis. It is divided into head, body or tail. The tail continues as vas deferens. It is the site for sperm maturation, where the sperms acquire motility. Epididymis is also the storage site for sperms and helps to propel them by contraction of vas deferens.

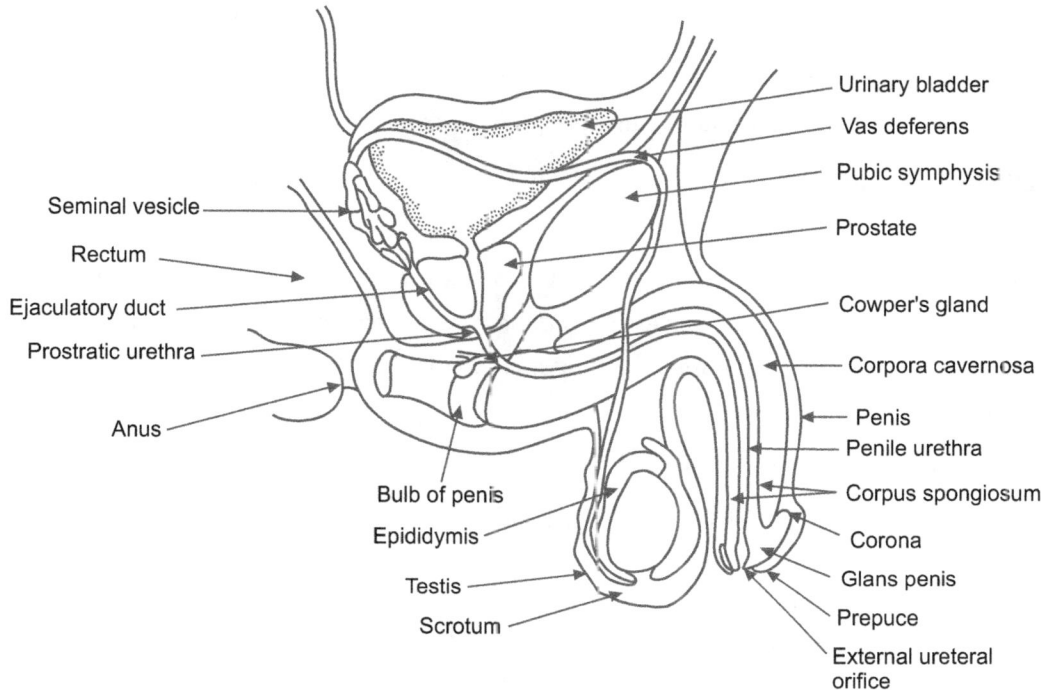

Figure 35.1 : Male reproductive system

Vas deferens : As the tail of epididymis continues, it leads to vas deferens, which is about 45 cm long; dilated part of vas deferens is called as ampulla.

Vas deferens stores and expels the sperm during ejaculation by contraction of muscular wall.

The urethra : It forms the terminal part of the duct of the reproductive and urinary system, and is the common pathway for semen and urine

The seminal vesicle : It is the accessory sex gland of the male. It consists of two pouch like structure, 4 -5 cm in length. Each seminal vesicle secretes a viscous alkaline fluid which contains fructose for ATP production by spermatozoa. Each seminal vesicle communicates to form ejaculatory duct. Fluid secreted by seminal vesicle normally constitutes about 60% of the total volume of semen.

Prostate gland : Prostate gland is located in the pelvic cavity anteriorly to the rectum. The prostate gland secretes milky alkaline fluid, which aid in lubrication during intercourse. It composed of citric acid, proteolytic enzyme and constitutes about 25% of total volume of semen.

Bulbourethral gland : This gland situated inferior to prostate on the either side of membranous urethra. It secretes alkaline fluid into urethra in sexual stimulation. It also secretes mucus that helps in lubricating the penis during intercourse.

Pathological significance

Cryptorchidism : It is a condition in which testes remain at undescended position in the inguinal ring, sometimes in abdomen. Crytorchidism may occur due to short spermatic cord, narrow inguinal canal, adhesion to peritoneal or inadequate testosterone secretion. Cryptorchidism may result in infertility, inguinal hernia and malignancy.

Elephantiasis : It is the thickening of scrotum skin which looks look elephant's hide, leading to enlargement of scrotum.

Prostatitis : It is the inflammation of prostate gland occurs commonly due to bacterial infection mainly through urethral route.

EXERCISE

1. Enlist the various male reproductive organs with their functions.
2. Give the anatomy and physiology of testis.
3. What is the function of epidydimis?
4. What is cryptorchidism?

EXPERIMENT NO. 36

STUDY OF THE FEMALE REPRODUCTIVE SYSTEM

➢ Aim

To study the female reproductive system.

➢ Theory

Female reproductive system consists of ovaries, fallopian tubes, vagina, vulva (external genital organs) and breasts (figure 36.1).

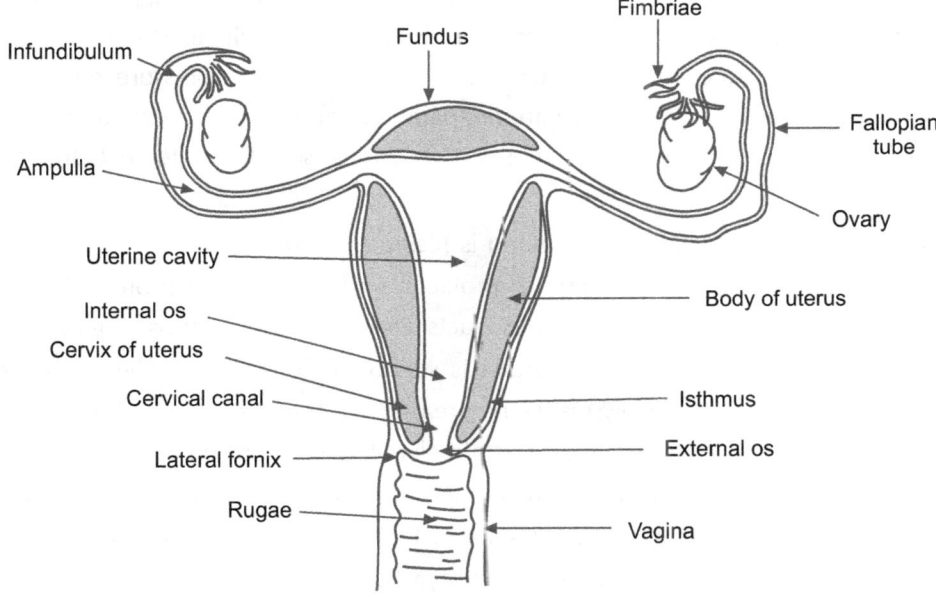

Figure 36.1 : Female reproductive tract

Vagina : It is a tube lined structure, 10-12 cm long that begins from the cervical region of the uterus. It functions as a passage for the foetus at the time of delivery, menstrual blood during menses and sperms during sexual intercourse. A recess called fornix is attached to the cervix on which the intrauterine devices (contraceptive device) especially diaphragm are placed. Vaginal smooth muscles adequately stretch during child birth and intercourse. The superficial layer of the vagina, called the adventia is composed of connective tissue. At the vaginal orifice, there is a thin membrane called hymen, forming border of the orifice (os) that get ruptured during intercourse.

Vulva : It includes the following structures-

Mons pubis : It is anterior to the urethral and vaginal openings and is composed of adipose tissue, covered with skin and pubic hair.

Labia majora : These are two folds extending from mons pubis, to the perineum. It is made up of adipose tissue, sebaceous glands, and sweat glands with pubic hair.

Labia minora: These are two folds on both side of the vagina composed of fatty tissue, sebaceous glands and sweat glands.

Clitoris : It is located anterior to the labia minora. It is a cylindrical mass of erectile tissue. The stimulation of clitoris produces sexual excitement in female.

Vestibule : It is the space between the labia minora (inner labia or vaginal lips, flaps of skin on either side of the vaginal opening and is surrounded by labia majora) and is occupied by the vaginal orifice, the hymen and the urethral orifice. This tissue helps to narrow the vaginal orifice during sexual intercourse which puts pressure on the penis. Within the urethra and vaginal orifice are the paraurethral mucus secretion and bartholins gland respectively. These glands secrete mucus during sexual excitement and aids in lubrication during intercourse.

Breasts (mammary glands) : This gland is responsible for synthesis and expression of milk under the influence of hormone viz; prolactin and oxytocin. Each breast has nipple, behind which are present the lactiferous ducts and sebaceous glands. Pigmented area around the nipple is the areola .The breast is supported by supensory ligaments, which pass through the skin lying deeply inside the breast. Each breast has 20-25 lobes separated by adipose tissue .The lobules of breast contain alveoli and is surrounded by myoepithelial cells. Contraction of these cells under the influence of oxytocin (a hormone released from the posterior lobe of pituitary gland) results in the expression of milk. Lactation is the process of synthesis and ejection of milk from breasts.

Ovaries : These are two in number which produce sex hormones (estrogen and progesterone)and the ova. Each ovary lies in the shallow cavity on the lateral wall of the pelvis attached to uterus by broad ligament called as mesovarium. Each ovary measures about 2-4 cm in length, 2 cm in breath and is 1.20 to 1.40 cm thick, consisting of fibrous tissue, blood and lymphatic vessels, nerves etc (figure 36.2).

Fallopian tubes : These are two in number, lying one on each lateral side of fundus of the uterus. Each tube measures about 10 cm long. These tubes are responsible for transport of ovum towards the uterus. The funnel shaped region of fallopian tube is known as in infundibulum. The infundibulum has finger like projections. The fallopian tube is made up of three layers of viz. serosa, muscularis and mucosa which help in the movement of the fertilised ovum. Also due to peristaltic action of the muscularis, ovum is propelled along the tube.

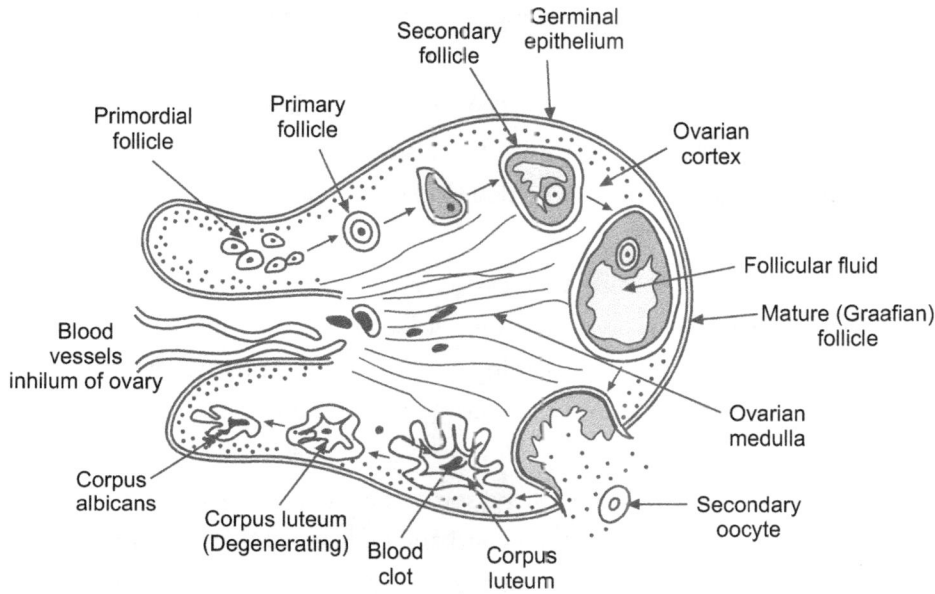

Figure 36.2 : Ovary

Uterus : Uterus is present between the bladder and rectum. It is the site for implantation of fertilised ovum, development of the embryo and foetus and also a passage for menstrual bleeding. It is a pear shaped organ having 7.5 to 8 cm long, 5 cm wide and 2.5 cm thick having fundus, body and cervix. Uterine cavity is the space between the uterine walls. Uterus also has three layers, outer layer is perimetrium, myometrium (middle having smooth muscle) and endometrium. Myometrium produces coordinated contraction under the influence of oxytocin during labor, helps expulsion of foetus from the uterus. Endometrium has two important layers, stratum functionalis and baselis. Stratum functionalis sloughs off (rupture) at the onset of menstruation while stratum basilis gives rise to formation of new stratum functionalis after menstrual bleeding.

> **Pathological significance**

Dysmenorhea : Pain during menstruation occurs due to tumour, formation of ovarian cysts, pelvic inflammatory disorder, intrauterine devices, oral contraceptive usage etc.

Pelvic inflammatory disease : Bacterial infection of pelvic organs (uterus, uterine tube, ovaries) characterised by pelvic soreness, lower back pain, abdominal pain etc

Vulvovaginal candidiasis : It is characterised by itching, thick yellowish vaginal discharge, pain, and commonly occurs due to fungal infection with *Candida albicans*. Antifungal drugs like Fluconazole are commonly used for treatment of candidiasis infection due to *Candida albicans*.

Polycystic ovarian syndrome (PCOS) : This syndrome is characterised by oligomenorrhoea, anovulation, infertility, hirsutism and obesity in young female with enlarged and cystic ovaries. This may be due to excess androgen secretion and less follicle stimulating hormones.

Dysfunctional uterine bleeding : Excessive bleeding during or in between menstrual periods without a causative uterine lesion. It occurs commonly in association with anvolutary cycle i.e. menarche (beginning of the cycle) and menopause (cession of menstrual cycle). Anovulation occurs due to hyper secretion of estrogen alone without progesterone.

Premenstrual syndrome : It is cystic disorder characterised by edema, weight gain, breast swelling, pain, constipation, anxiety, irritability, headache, etc. A complete and diet with carbohydrates, proteins, fibre and analgesic drugs (ibuprofen or diclofenac sodium) can reduce the severity of this disorder.

Endometriosis : It is a condition in which cells from the lining of the endometrial layer grow outside the uterine cavity and is characterised by symptoms such as bleeding, severe pain during menstruation and infertility. The main sites for abnormal endometrial development are ovaries, uterine ligaments, rectovaginal septum, pelvic peritoneum, vagina, vulva, etc.

EXERCISE

1. Enlist the various organs of the female reproductive tract
2. Describe the anatomy of the ovary
3. Define the following terms
   (a) Endometriosis,
   (b) Dysmenorrhea,
   (c) Polycystic ovarian syndrome,
   (d) Premenstrual syndrome.

EXPERIMENT NO. 37

STUDY OF THE HUMAN EYE

➤ Aim

To study the human eye.

➤ Theory

The eye is a special organ for the sense of sight. It is located in the orbital cavity; it is spherical in shape and 2.5 cm in diameter. The eye ball measures about 2.5cm diameter. The orbit of the eye is formed by different bones which protect the eye ball. Anatomically, the wall of the eye ball is divided into 3 layers. Outer layer is a fibrous coat; consisting of sclera and cornea, the middle layer is a vascular coat consisting of choroid, ciliary body and iris. The inner layer known as retina consists of nervous tissue (Figure 37.1).

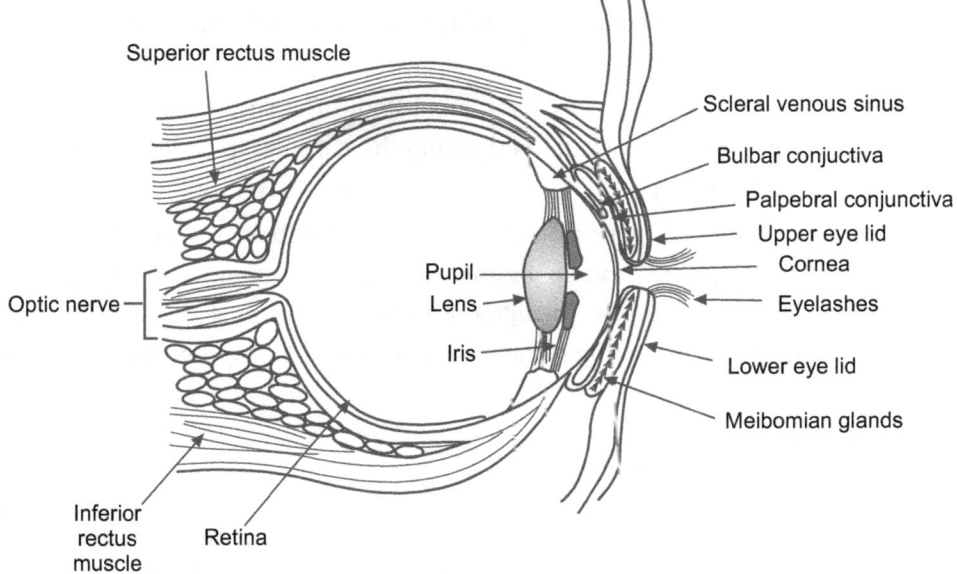

Figure 37.1 : The Human Eye

1. **Sclera :** The white region of eye is made up of collagen fibers and fibroblast. The fibrous tissue of sclera maintains the shape of the eye and also provides site for attachment to the extrinsic muscles of the eye.

2. **Cornea :** It is 0.5-1.0 cm thick, made up of epithelium, it functions in transmission light toward retina as well as provides effective barrier against bacterial invasion.
3. **Choroid :** It is situated posterior to the sclera and is very vascular, deep chocolate brown in colour. Light enters the eye through activating the nerve ending in the retina and finally absorbed by choroid.
4. **Ciliary body :** Presents anteriorly to the choroid, consists of the non – striated muscle fibers, epithelial cells and contains ciliary process. Secretion from epithelial cells forms aqueous humor. The size of pupil changes due to contraction and relaxation of ciliary muscles under postsynaptic stimulation and occulomotor nerve.
5. **The iris :** It is anterior to ciliary body, between the cornea and lens, consists of circular and radial smooth muscles. At the centre of the iris is the pupil; the size of the pupil changes during contraction of circular muscle and radial muscle. Circular muscle has parasympathetic innervations and upon activation it contracts (meiosis) and the size of pupil reduces; this is observed in bright light. In bright light, the sympathetic nerve innervates the radial muscle and its activation leads to relaxation of radial muscle (mydriasis).
6. **Lens :** It is a circular- biconvex transparent body. The suspensory ligaments of the ciliary body holds the lens enclosed within the capsule. It is elastic in nature and lies posterior to the pupil.
7. **Retina :** It lines in the inner surface of the choroid and is composed of nerve cells fibers. They acts as rods and cones and are activated depending upon the intensity of light passing into the eye. The vitreous humour in the eyeball cavity, posterior to the lens, helps in maintaining intraocular pressure to support the retina against choroid.

➢ Physiology of vision

Photoreceptors and photo pigments – Stimulation/ activation of the photo receptors takes place when the image of the object is focused on retina, thereby transfering light to bipolar cells. The rhodopsin of rod and other pigments of cones are responsible for colour vision.

Optic tracts : It is the pathway posterior to the optic chiasma. The tract consists of nasal fibers of retina. The tract goes back side to meet lateral geniculature into the cerebrum. Lateral geniculate situated posterior and lower to the thalamus and is the relay center for visual information received from the retina of the eye. It collects information from the ascending retinal ganglion cells through the optic tract and from the reticular activating system and thus neurons sends their axons via optic radiation.

Pathological significance

Cataract : It is the clouding of the lens inside the eye which leads to decrease in vision. It is the most common cause of blindness and is conventionally treated with surgery.

Glaucoma : It is a group of ocular disorders with multi-factorial etiology, characteristic with increase in intraocular pressure-associated optic neuropathy that results in impairment in vision.

Cycloplegia : It is paralysis of the ciliary muscle of the eye, resulting in loss of accommodation.

EXERCISE

1. Give the anatomy of the human eye.
2. What is the role of retina?
3. Give the physiology of vision.
4. Describe the following
   (a) Cataract
   (b) Glaucoma
   (c) Cycloplegia

EXPERIMENT NO. 38

STUDY OF THE HUMAN EAR

➤ Aim

To study the human ear

➤ Theory

Ear is the organ of hearing. The cranial nerve (8th cranial nerve) carries sensation of hearing towards the cerebral cortex which is a region for the integration and interpretation of information.

Ear is divided into 3 regions

External Ear : Collects sound waves and transmits towards middle ear.

Middle Ear : Middle ear also called as tympanic ear, which conveys sound vibrations to the oval window

Internal Ear : Receives and interprets the sound for hearing and equilibrium.

External ear : Consists of the following parts.

Pinna OR Auricle : It is the expanded part, made up of fibroblastic cartilage covered with skin. The expanded outer edge is known as helix and lower most part is the lobule. Ligaments and muscle attach the pinna to the head.

External auditory canal : It is an irregular shaped long tube about 2.5cm in length which lies in the temporal bone and leads from auricle to the ear drum. It is divided into cartilaginous and osseous part. Cartilaginous part is about 1/3rd of auditory and contains ceruminous glands which secrete wax called cerumen that helps to trap the entry of unwanted particles into the ear.

Middle ear : It is small and filled with air and is known as tympanic cavity. The middle ear contains a chain of three small bones called auditory ossicles of which one end is connected to the ear drum and other end to fenestra vestibuli. Auditory ossicles also contain malleus, incus and stapes (figure 38).

The handle of the malleus attaches to the internal surface of the ear drum. The hand of the malleus articulates with the head of stapes. The base of the stapes fits into the oval window.

Internal ear : Internal ear is bony and in the form of a membranous labyrinth. The space between two labyrinths contain perilymph fluid, whereas, membranous labyrinth contains endolymph fluid.

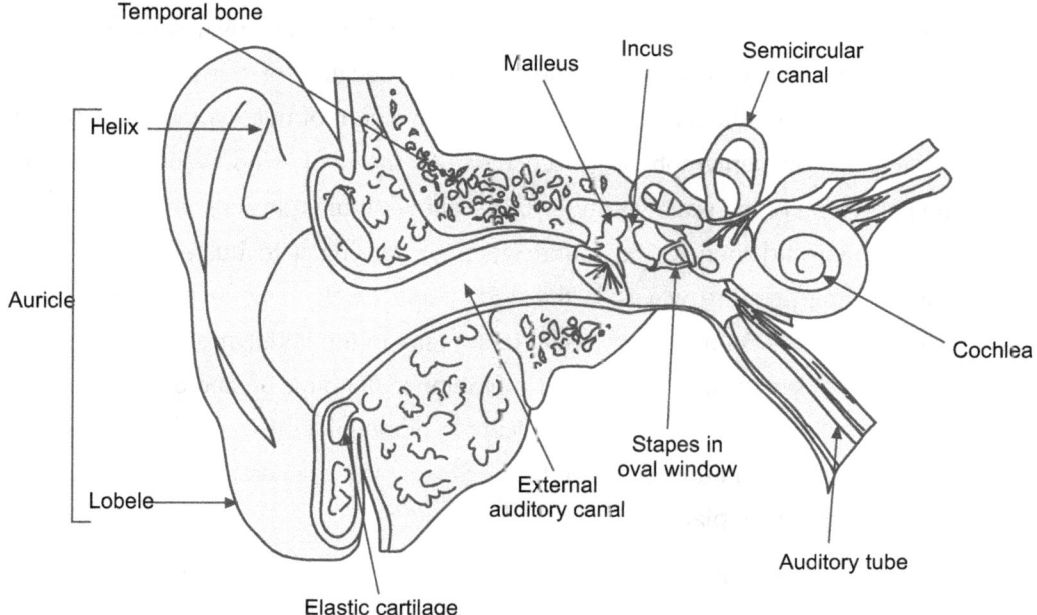

Figure 38.1 : The ear

The bony labyrinth is divided into 3 parts

Vestibule is an expanded part of the middle of ear contains fenestra vestibule and cochlea.

The cochlea is snail shaped organ having broad base and apex. The three canals are continuous with the vestibule. The membranous labyrinth in the vestibules consists of sac called utricle and saccule which are connected by small ducts.

At one end of each semicircular canal is a swollen enlargement called the ampulla. The vestibular branch of the vestibulocochler nerve (13th cranical nerve) consists of ampullary, utricular and saccular nerves. Cell bodies of the sensory neurons are located in vestibular ganglia. Auditory nerve goes posteriorly through temporal bone and reaches the hearing area of the cerebral cortex.

> **Physiology of hearing**

The auricle or pinna collects the sound waves and transmits them into the external auditory canal, where it strikes the ear drum. Because of the change in the pressure of air, the ear drum vibrates. The central area of the ear drum connects to malleus, which also vibrates. These vibrations are transferred to incus and in turn to stapes. As the stapes vibrate, the membrane of oval window is pushed in and out. The oval window vibrates about 20 times more vigorously than the ear drum because of transmission of small vibration oscillates over a larger surface area. The movement of oval window sets up fluid pressure waves in the perilymph of the cochlea. As the oval window bulges ahead, it pushes the perilymph of the scala vestibuli. The scala vestibule transmits pressure waves to the scala tymphani and then to the round window, causing it to bulge outward in the middle ear building pressure waves in the endolymph (rich in potassium ions) present inside the cochlear duct. Vibration of basilar membrane in the endolymph, allows hair cell movement of spiral organ against tectorial membrane. Bending of stereocilia (mechano sensing organelles of hair cells)leads to receptor potential which results in the nerve impulse formation through auditory nerve to hearing area of the cerebral cortex where the interpretation of wave take place.

➢ Pathological significance

Deafness : hearing impairment, or hearing loss is a partial or total inability to hear.

Otitis : Inflammation of ear due to infection.

EXERCISE

1. Enlist the various parts of ear
2. Give the anatomy of the ear.
3. Give the physiology of hearing.
4. What is deafness?

EXPERIMENT NO. 39

STUDY OF THE HUMAN SKIN

➢ Aim

To study the human skin

➢ Theory

Skin is part of the integumentary system which helps in protection and temperature regulation. It is also known as cutaneous membrane, an outer covering of body with surface area of about 1.5-2 m^2 and consists of glands, hairs and various cells. Skin has two important layers i.e. epidermis and dermis (Figure 39.1).

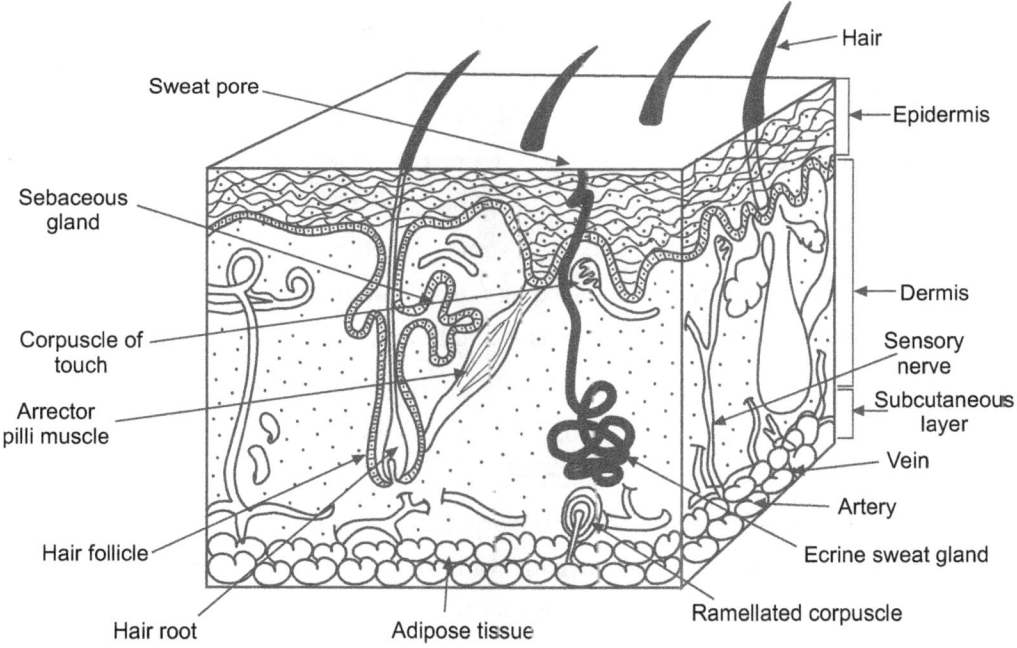

Figure 39.1 : The Human Skin

Epidermis : It is the superficial layer of the skin, made up of stratified keratinized squamous epithelium which varies in thickness in different parts of the body. Blood vessels and nerve endings are absent in the epidermis, although for supply of oxygen and nutrients, deeper layer are bathed in the interstitial fluid of the dermis.

The keratinocytes, melanocytes, Langerhans and markel cells are the important cells found in the epidermis. Keratinocytes produce a protein called as keratin which helps in protection from heat, chemicals and microorganism. Melanocytes are cells which produce a pigment known as melanin which gives a characteristic colour to the skin and protect skin from UV light. Lagerhans cells originate from the bone marrow, migrate towards the epidermis and prevent the entry of microorganisms into the skin. Merkel cells formed deep in the epidermis detect touch sensation. Epidermis is made up of stratum basale, stratum lucidum, stratum spinosum, stratum corneum, stratum granulosum.

Stratum basale is made up of cuboidal columnar ketatinocytes, which form a tough protein keratin which helps in protection from injury to deeper layer. Stratum spinousm superficial to stratum basale gives strength and flexibility to the skin. Stratum granulosum, a middle portion of epidermis is made up of 3-5 flattened keratinocytes, the keratinocytes acts water repellent sealant, retard loss and entry of water and foreign materials. During apoptosis (programmed cell death), break down of nuclei take place, and thus keratinocytes of stratum granulosum do not carry out metabolic reactions and they die. Hence, stratum granulosum marks the trasition between the deeper, metabolically active strata and the dead cells of the superficial strata. Stratum lucidum found in fingertips, palms of hands and sole of feet provides toughness. Stratum corneum is the outer layer of epidermis offers protection to microorganisms and injury.

Dermis : It is a tough, elastic layer made up of dense irregular connective tissue - collagen fibre. The different cells found in the dermis are fibroblasts, macrophages, adipocytes along with blood vessels, nerves, glands and hair follicles. Dermis is divided into papillary and reticular region. The papillary region is made up of collagen and elastic fibres, and perceives the sensation of pain, warmth, cold, tickling and itching, whereas, reticular region consists of fibroblasts, macrophages, and adipocytes. The network like arrangement of collagen fibers helps the skin resist stretching. Collagen and elastic fibers provides the skin with strength, flexibility and ability to stretch.

Sweat glands : These are distributed throughout the skin, predominantly found in the palms of hands, soles of feet, axillary and groin regions. Tiny pours of sweat gland secrete clear, watery fluid; due to decomposition of bacteria it has unpleasant smell.

Hair : These are present on skin surface except on the palms and soles of feet. Hair is divided into shaft (above the skin) and root (portion that penetrates into the dermis and up to the subcutaneous layer). Hair follicles are the part surrounding the root and made up of epithelial root sheath. The onion shaped structure at the base of each hair follicle is known as bulb, which contains a nipple shaped serration called papilla, made up of areolar connective tissue and blood vessels responsible for nourishment for hair follicles.

Sebaceous glands : These are found in the skin of the scalp, face, axillae and groin region.Theysecrete sebum into hair follicles and thus keep the hair soft with shiny appearance and prevent infection against bacteria and fungi. Sebum also prevents drying and cracking of the skin. During puberty, there is excessive secretion of sebaceous glands rendering the skin prone to the effects of excessive moisture.

➢ **Functions of skin**

1. Provides protection against microorganisms and UV light.
2. Regulates body temperature by maintaining homeostasis
3. Synthesis of vitamin D through exposure to UV light;
4. Prevent dehydration due to moisturizing action.

EXERCISE

1. Enlist the layers of skin.
2. Discuss in short the structure of skin.
3. Give the role of epidermis.
4. Enlist the various functions of skin.
5. Enlist the various cells present in skin.

EXPERIMENT NO. 40

PREGNANCY DIAGNOSTIC TEST

➤ Aim

To perform the pregnancy diagnostic test

➤ Requirements

Readymade pregnancy detection kit, urine of pregnant women (preferably collected in the morning), dropper etc.

➤ Principle

This test is based on the principle of development of pink colour (use readymade kit or strips) or agglutination i.e. clumps of antigen- antibody (antiserum of hCG). The human chorionic gonadotrophic (hCG) a hormone secreted from the trophoblast after 6 days of fertilisation (fusing of sperm and ova in the fallopian tubes), is necessary for the maintenance of corpus leutem and to continue the progesterone secretion at the beginning of pregnancy. The concentration of hCG is high approximately about 8-10 IU/ml during the first three months of pregnancy and drastically decreases from the 4th month onward of pregnancy.

➤ Procedure

1. The approximate level of hCG in urine for sensitivity is 1.5-3.5 IU/ml in the slide test and 0.2-1.2 IU/ml in tube test.

   This concentration of hCG is achieved after the 6- 8th day of fertilisation. Hence, it is performed after 6-8th days of fertilization.

2. Collect the first urine sample of a pregnant woman in the morning in a clean vial.

3. Add 1-2 drops of urine sample on hCG antisera plate (in case of strip, dip it into vial of urine sample up to the test mark) and wait for 5-10 minutes.

4. Record the observation as per the following figures and note whether pregnancy test is positive or negative.

5. The appearance of pink color indicates positive test whereas (figure 40.1), no colour indicates negative test.

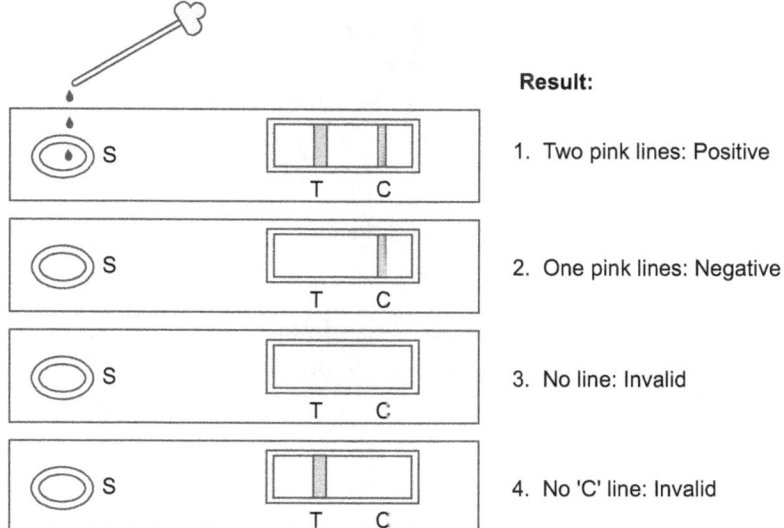

Figure 40.1: Pregnancy detection test showing positive (1) negative (2) and invalid (3 & 4) results

EXERCISE

1. Give the principle of pregnancy detection test.
2. Give the normal sensitivity of hCG in urine.
3. Give the role of hCH in pregnancy.

❖❖❖

EXPERIMENT NO. 41

STUDY OF FAMILY PLANNING METHODS AND DEVICES

➤ **Aim**

To study the family planning methods and devices

➤ **Theory**

Family planning allows people to have desired number of children and determine the spacing of pregnancies. It is achieved through use of contraceptive methods and the treatment of infertility. Family planning refers to practices that help couple to attain certain objectives

- To delay pregnancy, space pregnancies or prevent pregnancy.
- To help prevent the transmission of HIV and other sexually transmitted infections (use of condoms).
- Family planning reduces the need for unsafe abortions.
- Family planning reinforces people's rights to determine the number and spacing of their children.

➤ **Methods of family planning**

1. Behavioral method
2. Natural method
3. Chemical method
4. Hormonal method

1. **Behavioral method**

   (a) **Abstinence :** It is a self-enforced restraint from sexual intercourse. It is 100 % effective in preventing conception. However, not everyone who intends to be abstinent refrains from all sexual activity.

   (b) **Coitus interrupts :** It is method of voluntary fertility control, which is also known as the rejected sexual intercourse, withdrawal or pull-out method. It is a method of birth-control in which a man, during intercourse withdraws his penis to prevent the deposition of semen having sperm into the vagina. The man then directs his ejaculate (semen) away from his partner's vagina in an effort to avoid insemination.

   (c) **Periodic method (safe period for intercourse) :** This is known as calendar method or rhythmic method. It is calculation-based approach where previous menstrual cycles are used to expect the first and the last fertile day in future menstrual cycles.

It is based on the regularity of the menstrual cycle and the fact that an ovum (egg) can only be fertilised within 24 hours of ovulation. In normal menstrual cycle, avoidance of intercourse between 12-18th day (occurrence of bleeding is 1st day of menstrual cycle) prevents fertilisation, as ovulation take place on the 14th day. Sperms survive for nearly about 2-3 days in vagina and ovum survives for only one day. Therefore, 1st -10th, 19th -27th days are safe periods to prevent fertilisation and days 12th -18th are unsafe.

2. **Natural method**

This method is as safe as that of the rhythmic method. In this method, self recognition of physiological sign and symptoms by female related to events of ovulation, during which intercourse must be avoided

   (a) **Basal body temperature :** At the time of ovulation, the body temperature rises by 0.3-0.6^{0}C due to progesterone production. This method is reliable if intercourse in avoided during the post ovulatory period (3 days after the ovulation).

   (b) **Cervical mucous method :** As ovulation begins, mucus becomes watery clear, similar to egg white, slippery. After ovulation, it becomes thick, and its secretion is reduced.

3. **Chemical method**

In this method, spermicidal agents which act as surface active agents kill the sperm deposited in the vagina during intercourse.

   (a) **Foam tablet :** It is inserted by the female into vagina before intercourse. Foaming action of these tablets forms a coating that kills the sperms released during ejaculation.

   (b) **Jelly or cream :** Contain spermicidal formulation which is applied with the help of applicator before intercourse.

   (c) **Condom :** It is a thin rubber tube unrolled on erect penis before intercourse, it covers the penis and thus prevents the direct discharge of semen containing sperm into the vagina (Figure 41.1).

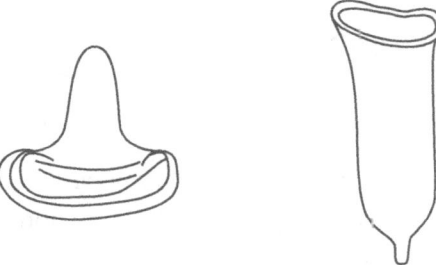

Figure 41.1: Condom

(d) Diaphragm : It is a vaginal barrier also called as Dutch cap. It is a thin, shallow, rubber cap, dome shaped with spring molded into the rim having diameter 50-10 cm. It is inserted deep into vagina before the intercourse and remains there up to 6-7 hrs after intercourse. Diaphragm blocks the opening of uterus which prevents the entry of sperm into uterus and thus no fertilisation occurs (Figure 41.2).

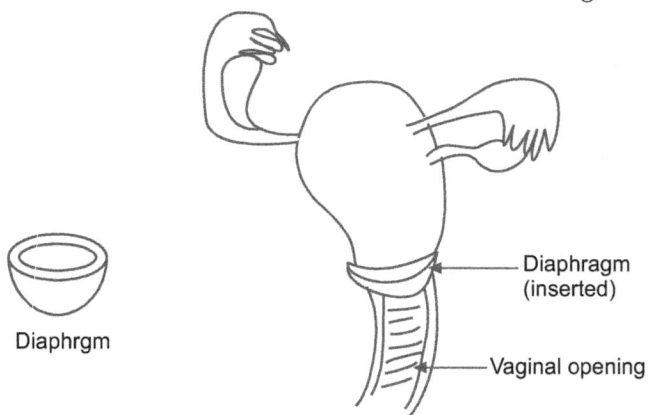

Figures 41.2 : Diaphragm

4. Hormonal method

It consists of progesterone and estrogen at a concentration of 0.5 mg and 30-35 µg respectively. Pill is taken orally for 21 consecutive days starting from 1st day of menstrual cycle, followed by 7 days placebo (without drug) during which bleeding occurs (Figure 41.3)

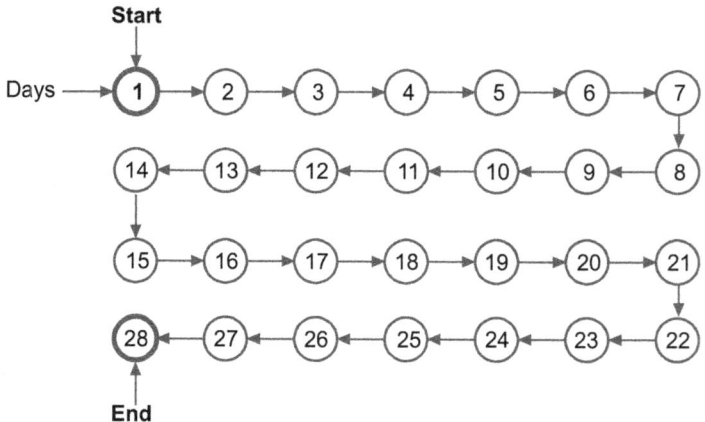

Pills for day 1 to 21 contain combination hormones (e.g. Levohorgestral and ethinylestradial). The remaining 7 pills contains no hormones (palcebo pills)

Figure 41.3 : Hormonal Pills

➤ Intrauterine devices (IUDs)

Intrauterine device is a small 'T'-shaped device, containing either copper or levonorgestrel, which is inserted into the uterus (figure 41.4). They are a form of long-acting reversible contraception, and the most effective type of reversible birth control.

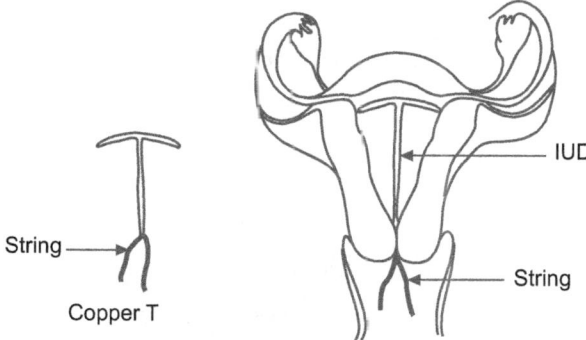

Figure 41.4: Copper 'T'

Copper T : This IUD is made up of plastic and wrapped with copper which enhances the effectiveness of this device.

Progetasert : This is a 'T' shaped device filled with progesterone which releases slowly into uterus at a concentration of 65 µg per day. It has local effect on uterine lining and cervical mucus.

5. Terminal method of contraception

Vasectomy : It is a simple surgical procedure to be performed in males and is 100 % effective. A small cut of 1 cm above the scrotum on both sides of vas deferens is given, separated and then sealed by suturing, or clamping to prevent sperm from entering into the seminal stream.

Tubectomy : It is a surgical procedure for permanent contraception to prevent future pregnancies in women. Cut is given on both the fallopian tubes.

EXERCISE
---

1. Give the objective of family planning.
2. Enlist the various methods of family planning.
3. Enlist the various chemical methods of family planning.
4. What are intrauterine devices? Give their mechanism of action.

EXPERIMENT NO. 42

BIOCHEMICAL ANALYSIS OF URINE

➢ Aim

To perform biochemical analysis of urine sample

➢ Requirements

Test tubes, test tube stand, holder, stirrer, and various chemical reagents

➢ Theory

Urine is a liquid by-product of the body excreted through the kidneys by the process of urination from the urethra. The body's waste products are mainly eliminated through urine. The total volume of urine excreted through kidneys in 24 hrs ranges from 800-3000 ml and varies from individual to individual and diseases conditions.

➢ Characteristic of urine

Volume	800-1800 mL/day (96% water and 4 % dissolved components
Colour	Pale yellow due to presence of urochrome
pH	6-7.4
Specific gravity	1.006-1.025
Odour	Aromatic and peculiar

Constituents of urine

Normal	Abnormal
1. **Inorganic** Calcium-0.05-0.31 mEq/kg, chloride- 6-9 gm, phosphate-0.5-1.4 gm, sulphate upto 1gm, bicarbonate-18-22 mmol/L and ammonia-20-50 mEq/24 hrs. 2. **Organic** Urea- 20-30 gm, uric acid 0.4-0.8 gm and creatinine 1-1.8 gm	Blood, glucose (sugar), proteins, ketone bodies, pus and pigments etc.

Qualitative analysis of urine sample

Parameters	Observation	Inference
Volume of urine	800-2000ml/day	Normal
	Less than 800 ml/day	Bacterial infection, dehydration, vomiting, less water intake, fever etc.
	More than 2000 ml/day	Polyuria (due to diabetes mellitus)
Colour	Pale yellow	Normal
	Reddish	Hematuria (presence of blood)
	Marked reddish	Reduced urine output
	Dark orange to brown	Jaundice
Odour	Unpleasant	Excretion of metabolites
pH	Below 6	Acidosis
	Above 7.6	Alkalosis
Turbidity	Cloudy	Bacterial infection, crystal of calcium

(A) ANALYSIS OF NORMAL CONSTITUENTS

A. Organic constituents

1. **Test for urea:** Take 5 ml urine sample, to it add 4-5 drops of phenolphthalein and pinch of soybean powder; it results in pink colour indicating the presence of urea.

2. **Test for uric acid :** Moisten the filter paper with urine sample and dip it into silver nitrate solution; if it turns yellowish brown it indicates the presence of urea.

3. **Test for creatinine:** Add 2 ml of sodium nitroprusside and 2 ml of 10 % NaOH in 10 ml of urine, a ruby red colour indicates the presence of creatinine.

B. Inorganic constituents

1. **Chloride ions :** Add 1 ml of conc. HNO_3 and 0.5 ml silver nitrate solution in 5 ml of urine sample. Presence of white curdy precipitate of silver chloride indicates the presence of chloride ions.

2. **Sulphate ions :** Add 2-3 drops of conc. HCl and 4-5 drops of barium chloride in urine sample and mix well. An opaque milky precipitate indicates the presence of sulphate ions.

3. **Bicarbonate ions :** Addition of dil. sulphuric acid to urine sample produces effervescences of CO_2 gases.

4. **Phosphate ions :** In 5 ml of urine sample add 5 ml of conc. nitric acid and ammonium molybdate, heat the solution. A canary yellow precipitate indicates the presence of phosphate ions in urine.

5. **Calcium ions:** Add 2-3 drops of NaOH, ammonium oxalate and 1 % acetic acid in urine sample. The appearance of white precipitate indicates the presence of calcium ions.

6. **Ammonia :** Add 40 % NaOH in urine sample, dip the red litmus paper. If it turns blue, ammonia is present.

(B) ANALYSIS OF ABNORMAL CONSTITUENTS

Blood

In 5 ml of urine sample, add benzidine powder and glacial acetic acid, mix and add hydrogen peroxide. Presence of a greenish blue colour indicates the presence of blood in urine.

Significance : Presence of blood in urine sample is known as hematuria, this may be due to tuberculosis, nephritis or urinary stone.

Sugar

Benedict test : In 5 ml of urine sample, add equal quantity of Benedict A and B solution and heat, cool it forms green to red precipitate indicating the presence of sugar (glucose).

Significance : Presence of sugar in urine sample is called as glycosuria; it is observed during diabetes mellitus.

Proteins

Addition of sulphosalicylic acid in urine produces white precipitate which indicates the presence of proteins.

Slow addition of conc. nitric acid in urine forms a white ring at junction which indicates the presence of proteins.

Significance : Presence of proteins in urine sample is known as proteinuria. The proteinuria is the indication of urinary tract infection, diet with excess protein and pregnancy.

Ketone bodies

To 5 ml of urine sample, add ammonium sulphate and sodium nitroprusside and 2-3 ml of strong ammonia slowly. Formation of permanganate colour indicates presence of ketone bodies.

Significance : Presence of ketone bodies in urine is called as ketonuria; this may be due to starvation, diabetes mellitus.

Bile salts

Add urine sample in a clean beaker and pour the sublimed sulphur powder on its surface, powder sinks to bottom which indicates the presence of bile salts in urine.

Significance : Presence of bile in urine is observed during obstructive jaundice.

Bile pigments

Add 1-2 drops of dil. HCl in 5 ml urine, filter the solution, dry the filter paper, pour the conc. nitric acid on filter paper, changes of colour from green to blue or violet to red and finally yellow indicates the presence of bile pigments.

Significance : Presence of bile pigments in urine is due to inflammation of liver.

EXERCISE

1. What is urine? Give the normal characteristics of urine.
2. Enlist various normal and abnormal constituents of urine.
3. Enlist the test for analysis of abnormal constituents of urine.
4. Give the significance of analysis of abnormal constitutes of urine.

EXPERIMENT NO.43

STUDY OF THE SIMPLE MUSCLE TWITCH

➤ Aim

To study the simple muscle twitch

➤ Requirements

Dissection box, kymograph, muscle trough (it is a plastic chamber used to keep the muscle live in ringer solution and having fixed electrode for muscle stimulation), induction coil, drum, Ringer solution, stimulating electrode, tuning fork for measuring different time intervals, thread, hook and weight.

➤ Principle

The stimulation of muscle with shock elicits the contraction called twitch. The twitch or contraction of muscle in response to electrical stimulation is known as simple muscle twitch and recording of this on kymograph is known as simple muscle curve.

Electrical stimulation of muscle results in contraction and this is recorded on kymograph with writing lever.

➤ Procedure

1. Arrange the primary and secondary circuit for recording the contraction of muscle as shown in figure 43.1.
2. Sacrifice the frog and dissect it, identify the sciatic nerve- gastrocnemius muscle (located with the soleus in the posterior (back) compartment of the leg). Fix it to muscle trough containing ringer solution.
3. Attach a load of 10 g weight as tension to the writing lever and adjust the writing lever in such a way that the pointer part of lever is slightly touching the rotating drum.
4. Place the writing lever with sketch pointer on white kymograph paper and record the baseline at 2.5 speed.
5. Apply the stimulus through the secondary coil for muscle contraction.
6. Press the tap key and release it as soon as contraction is recorded.
7. Vibrate the tuning fork by hitting on thigh and record a time trading below the simple muscle curve.
8. Stop the drum and close the circuiting key.

9. Keep the rotating drum in moving position for the contact arm to be touching the kymograph.

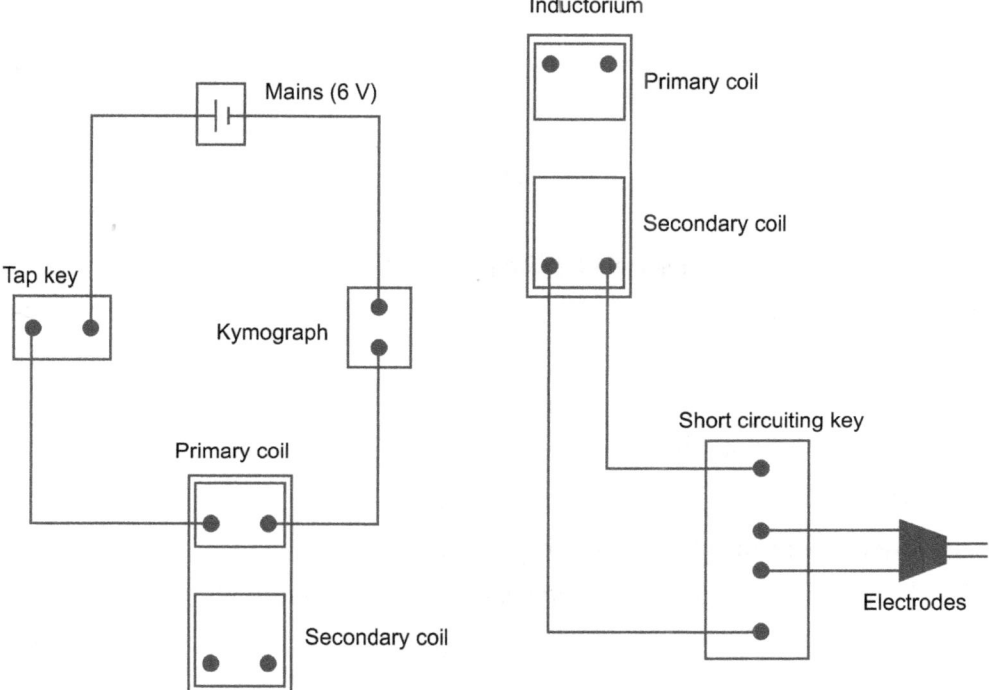

Figure 43.1 : Primary and secondary circuits

10. Mark the point of stimulation by rotating the drum (lever touching horizontally) so that it produces the tracing on the kymograph.
11. Record the total cycle consisting of beginning of contraction, peak and end of relaxation period.

➢ Observation

Prepare the simple muscle curve (figure 43.2) and calculate the contraction period, relaxation period and percentage of total muscle curve. The contraction period is the duration of contraction and it ranges from 20-40 ms. The relaxation period is the time taken by the muscle to produce relaxation. It is higher than contraction period and is usually in the range of 30-50 ms.

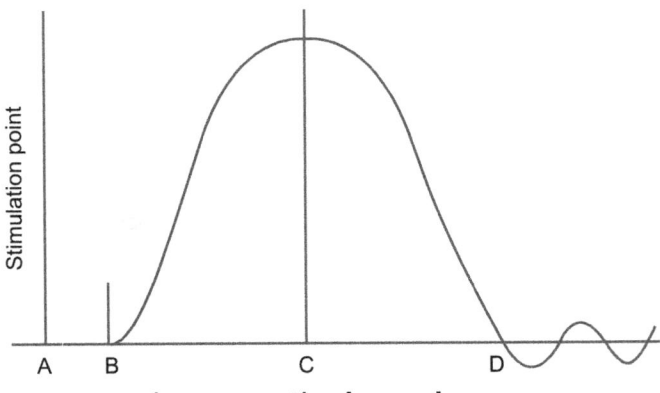

Figure 43.2: Simple muscle curve

Point A → B : latent period, B → C : Period of contraction, C → D : Period of relaxation

EXERCISE

1. What is simple muscle curve?
2. Define the contraction and relaxation period.
3. Give the principle of simple muscle twitch.
4. The load of 10 g is used for recording the contraction –justify

❖❖❖

EXPERIMENT NO. 44

EFFECT OF TEMPERATURE ON SIMPLE MUSCLE TWITCH

> **Aim**

To study the effect of temperature on simple muscle twitch

> **Requirements**

Similar assembly setup used for simple muscle twitch, Ringer solution with different temperature i.e. cold (8^0C), normal (27^0C) and warm (40^0C).

> **Principle**

The muscle contraction response is affected with change in temperature due to various factors, mainly biochemical and enzymatic alterations of tissues at a particular temperature.

> **Procedure**

1. Sacrifice the frog, dissect and isolate the sciatic nerve- gastrocnemius muscle.
2. Set up the assembly for recording of simple muscle curve as same as that of simple muscle twitch experiment.
3. Take simple muscle curve by recording the contraction using normal ringer solution with temperature of 27^0C.
4. Replace the normal ringer solution with warm solution (40^0C), keep it for 5-10 minutes and record the simple muscle curve.
5. Discard the warm solution, add normal ringer solution and replace with cold solution (8^0C) and repeat the same procedure.
6. Record the time tracing below the recording with the help of tuning fork.
7. Calculate the contraction and relaxation period at various temperatures at same base line (figure 44.1).

Observation table

Temperature of Ringer solution	Contraction period (ms)	Relaxation period (ms)	Height of contraction (cm)
Normal (27 °C)			
Warm (40 °C)			
Cold (8 °C)			

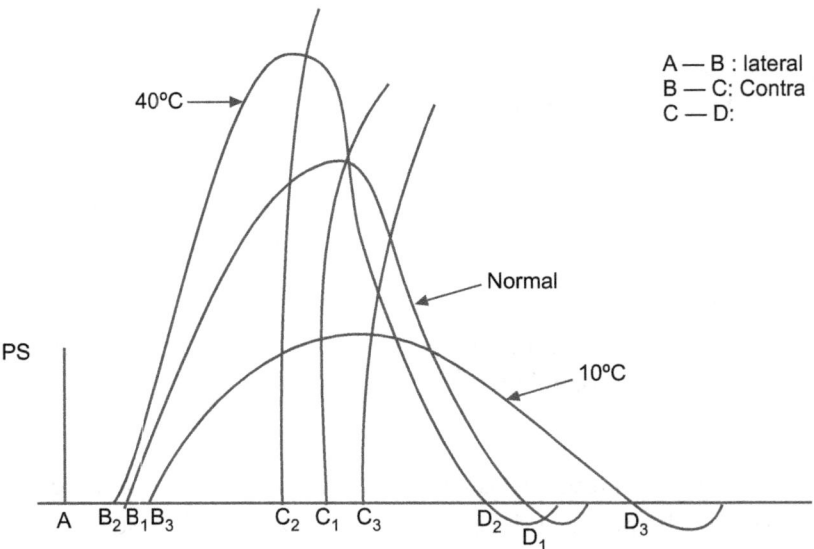

Figure 44.1 : Effect of temperature on simple muscle curve

➤ Significance

Alteration in temperature affects the muscle tonicity (contraction). The response of muscle at higher temperature (warm) results in decrease in latent, contraction and relaxation periods. This is because of higher conduction velocity, increased chemical transmission at neuromuscular junction (acetylcholine release in increases) and higher inertia of lever. The reduction in contraction period is also because of faster contraction of muscle and increase in enzymatic activity mainly ATPase. This results in increase in height/amplitude with contraction of muscle under the influence of high temperature.

The opposite effects can be observed with cold ringer solution due to reverse activity of ATPase and reduced neurochemical transmission.

EXERCISE

1. Give the principle involved in recording the effects of various temperatures on simple muscle curve.

2. Give the changes occurs on simple muscle twitch by using warm and cold ringer solution.

3. Explain why the contraction period is reduced at higher temperature?

❖❖❖

EXPERIMENT NO.45

STUDY OF FATIGUE ON GASTROCNEMIUS SCIATIC NERVE MUSCLE (OF FROG)

➤ Aim

To study the fatigue on the gastrocnemius sciatic nerve muscle preparation.

➤ Requirements

Similar assembly setup used for simple muscle twitch

➤ Principle

Fatigue is the transient inability of muscle to maintain optimal strength or performance i.e. reduces the performance due to continuous activity for longer period of time.

A muscle experiences fatigue when it is stimulated continuously for longer duration and this is recorded by stimulating the muscle at same baseline and the stimulation point.

➤ Procedure

1. Sacrifice the frog, dissect and locate the gastrocnemius sciatic nerve.
2. Mount the gastrocnemius sciatic nerve preparation in the muscle trough and set up the assembly for recording simple muscle curve and mark the point of stimulation.
3. Continue stimulating the sciatic nerve repeatedly and record the first, second and third contractions of muscle on speedy moving drum at the same stimulation point.
4. Shift the writing lever away from the drum
5. Keep on stimulating the gastrocnemius sciatic nerve preparation repeatedly at same stimulation point by keeping the tap key pressed and record every tenth contraction with lever touching the drum
6. Record the contraction until the muscle elicits fatigue (ensure by weak contraction i.e. reduce height and increased relaxation period.)
7. Further record the muscle contraction by changing the stimulation point at different places near the fatigue curve and at same base line.
8. Stimulate the muscle directly and record the contraction by changing stimulation point.
9. Replace the ringer solution with fresh solution and keep it for another 10 minutes.

10. Record the contraction at same baseline and change stimulation point near to previous base line.

➢ Observation

Contraction is recorded in terms of amplitude of contraction and duration of first three contraction and successive contractions. The onset of fatigue is ensured by the prolongation of relaxation period of muscle twitches and widening of base line as shown in figure 45.1(A) and (B). Further, contraction also takes place once the muscle is restored to normal position after the fatigue.

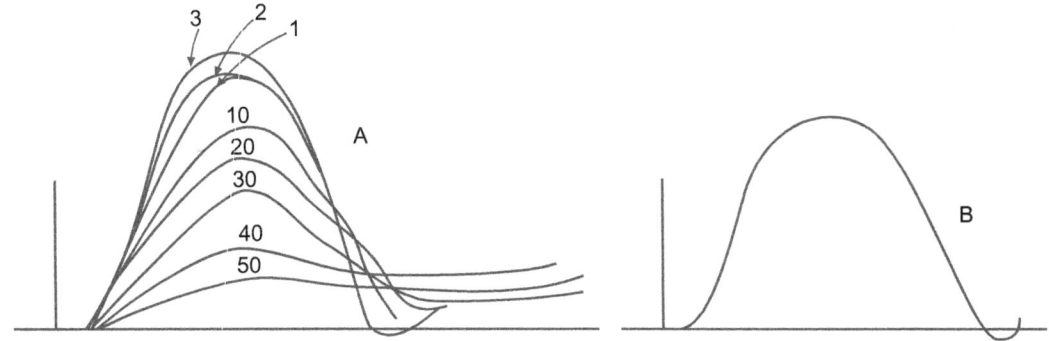

Figure 45.1 : Effect on fatigue on repetitive muscle stimulation (A) and after the fatigue (B)

➢ Significance

The fatigue in human being is determined by reduction in CNS activity and then physical performance (reduced neuromuscular transmission). The neuromuscular junction is the important site in which chemical transmission (acetylcholine released from nerve ending) take place and which initiate the skeletal muscle contraction. Hence, reduction in release of acetylcholine results in impaired muscle contraction.

EXERCISE

1. What is fatigue?
2. Give the principle involved in determination of fatigue on sciatic nerve muscle preparation.
3. Why does fatigue develop?

❖ ❖ ❖

APPENDIX

Normal values

Erythrocytes (RBCs)

    Female $3.9 - 5.2 \times 10^6/\mu L^3$

    Male $4.4 - 5.8 \times 10^6/\mu L^3$

Leukocytes (WBCs) $4.5-11.0 \times 10^3/mm^3$

    Lymphocytes :   16%-46% of white blood cells

    Monocytes   4-11% of white blood cells

    Neutrophils   45%-75% of white blood cells

Platelets (Thrombocytes) 150000-450000/ μL of blood

Haemoglobin (Hb)

    Male   13-18 g/dl

    Female   12-16 g/dl

    Children   11 to 16 g/dl

Glycosylated haemoglobin (HbA$_{1c}$) : 4-6.5 %

Normal blood PH   7.3

Blood pressure

    Systolic 120 mm of Hg

    Diastolic 80 mm of Hg

Blood glucose

    Fasting :70-105 mg/dl

    Post meal : less than 180 mg/dl

Total cholesterol : 150-200 mg/dl

    Total bilurubin :   0.2-1 mg/dl

    Creatinine :   0.5-1.5 mg/dl

Uric acid

    Male   4-6 mg/dl

    Female   3.5-6 mg/dl

Total proteins   6-8 g/dl
Urea   15-40 g/dl
Calcium   9-10 mg/dl

Gram - is the common measurement of weight used as pg (picograms), g (grams), mg (milligrams),

katal (kat) : micrometer (µm) : a unit of length. Mean Corpuscular Volume is expressed in cubic micrometers.

Mole : also "gram molecular weight," a quantity based on the atomic weight of the substance. Many test results in the Système Internationale are expressed as the number of moles per liter. In US units, these measurements are usually in grams per liter. Used in this table : mmol (millimoles), µmol, (micromoles), nmol (nanomoles), pmol (picomoles) per liter.

Micrometer (µm) : a unit of length. Mean Corpuscular Volume is expressed in cubic micrometers

Fractions and multipliers

deci (d) : 10^{-1} or ÷10

milli (m) : 10^{-3} or ÷1,000

micro (µ) : 10^{-6} or ÷1,000,000

nano (n) : 10^{-9} or ÷1,000,000,000

pico (p) : 10^{-12} or ÷1,000,000,000,00

GLOSSARY

Adipose tissue : This tissue consists of droplets of triglycerides which lie in subcutaneous layer of skin, heart, and kidney.

Agglutination : The clumping of cells such as bacteria or red blood cells in the presence of an antibody.

Anatomy : Study of the structure of living things including their systems, organs, and tissues. It includes the appearance and position of the various parts, and their relationships with other parts.

Anaemia : It is a decrease in the number of red blood cells (RBCs) or less than the normal haemoglobin (Hb) content in the blood.

Anosmia : It is characterised by inability of a person to smell.

Anterior : Located on or near the front of an organ.

Anticoagulants : These are the substances which prevent coagulation (clotting) of blood.

Arneth count: It describes the nucleus of a type of white blood cell called a neutrophil in an attempt to detect disease.

Asthma : It is a chronic inflammatory disease of the airways characterised by variable and recurring wheezing, coughing, chest tightness, and shortness of breath, reversible airflow obstruction, and bronchospasm.

Atherosclerosis : It is a condition in which an artery wall thickens due to accumulation of cholesterol and triglyceride.

Axilla or Armpit : The small hollow beneath the arm where it joins the body at the shoulders.

Bilateral : Related to both sides of body.

Bleeding time : The time required for the bleeding to cease is estimated to the nearest half minute.

Blood : It is a connective tissue consisting of RBC, WBC, and platelets

Bradycardia : It is a slow resting heart rate, pulse rate are below 60 beats / min.

Breath holding time : It is the time taken by an individual to hold his/her breath as long as possible

Caecum : A blind pocket like part that attaches the large intestine to ileum, a terminal part of the small intestine.

Caudal : Of, at, or near the tail or hind parts.

Cell : It is the basic structural, functional and biological unit of living microorganisms.

Cerumen : A secretion from ceruminous glands of ear.

Cheyne-stroke respiration : It is characterised by alternative apnea (difficulty in breathing) and hyperventilation.

Chorionic : The outer membrane enclosing the embryo.

Cilia : The slender protuberances that project from the much larger cell body

Clitoris : A erectile organ of the female that lies near to labia minora.

Clotting time : It is the time required for a sample of blood to coagulate in vitro under standard conditions.

Condom : It is a barrier device commonly used during sexual intercourse to reduce the probability of pregnancy and spread of sexually transmitted diseases.

Congenital heart diseases : It is the most common type of birth defect and is associated with different problems affecting the heart.

Deoxyribonucleic acid (DNA) : It is a molecule that encodes the genetic instructions used in the development and functioning of all known living organisms and many viruses.

Diaphragm : It is a small rubber dome placed in the vagina to wall off the cervix, thus preventing sperm from entering

Diarrhoea : The increase in frequency, volume and fluid content of the feces due to intestinal hyper motility

It is a symptom of various illnesses and bowel disturbances during which someone passes more frequent, loose, watery stools resulting in loss of electrolytes

Diastole : Relaxation of heart

Distal : Located far from a point of attachment.

Epithelial tissues : Tissues that line the cavities and surfaces of structures throughout the body, and also form many glands.

Erythropoiesis : It is a process of RBC (erythrocytes) formation or production

Erythropoietin : It is a hormone that controls erythropoiesis process.

Fever : It is elevation of body temperature due to bacterial or viral infection.

Granulocytes are white blood cells characterised by the presence of granules in their cytoplasm. They are of 3 types based on their staining property viz neutrophils, basophils and eosinophils.

Hematocrit : It is the volume percentage (%) of red blood cells in blood. Hematocrit also known as packed cell volume or erythrocyte volume fraction.

Haemoglobin : It is a protein in red blood cells that carries oxygen towards cells and tissues.

Hemolysis : It is the breakdown of red blood cells and the release of their contents into surrounding fluid.

Heparin : It is an anticoagulant effective in preventing deep vein thrombosis and pulmonary emboli (blockade of pulmonary artery).

Hepatitis : It is inflammation of the liver caused due to viral infection, drugs, alcohol and chemicals.

Hormones : They are the chemical substances released by a cell, a gland, or an organ in one part of the body that affects cells of other parts.

Hypertension : Sustained increase in arterial blood pressure above 80/120 mm of Hg.

Hyperthermia : It is elevated body temperature due to failed thermoregulation that occurs when a body produces or absorbs more heat than it disperses.

Inferior : Located at lower position or closer to the bottom or base.

Inflammation : It is a biological response of vascular tissues to harmful stimuli, such as pathogens, damaged cells, or irritants and characterised by pain, heat, redness, swelling, and loss of function.

Ischemia: A restriction in blood supply to tissues, causing a shortage of oxygen and glucose needed for cellular metabolism.

Jaundice: Yellowish colouration of the skin, conjunctival membranes (whites of the eyes), and other mucous membranes due to excess release of bilirubin, a pigment of liver.

Larynx : An organ commonly called the voice box, is located in the neck involved in breathing, sound production, and protecting the trachea against food aspiration

Lateral : Located on the left and right sides

Leukemia : It is a type of cancer of the blood or bone marrow characterised by an abnormal increase of immature white blood cells.

Leukocytosis : It is a white blood cell count greater than the normal range in the blood.

Leukopenia : A term used to denote a decrease in the number of white blood cells less than normal range found in the blood.

Lymph : It is the fluid that circulates throughout the lymphatic system.

Lymphocytes : These are white blood cells which determine the specificity of the immune response to infectious microorganisms and other foreign substances.

Macrophages : The differentiation of monocytes in tissues results in formation of macrophages. They engulf and then digest, cellular debris and pathogens.

Microscope : It is an instrument used to see objects that are too small for the naked eye.

Mitochondria : It is a membrane-enclosed structure found in most eukaryotic cells

Myopia : It is characterised by light rays coming from outside directly focus in front of retina, results in difficulty for person to see the distant object

Myxedema : It is a specific form of cutaneous and dermal edema secondary to increased deposition of glycosaminoglycans, hyaluronic acid, and other mucopolysaccharides.

Neutrophils : These are white blood cells, and the first immune cells to arrive at a site of infection or inflammation.

Olfaction : Sensation of smell.

Olfactory reference syndrome : It is the psychological disorder due to which patient imagines that he/she has strong body odour.

Osmosis : Movement of solvent molecules through a partially permeable membrane into a region of higher concentration, to the region of lower concentration until the equilibrium takes place.

Pathological : Involving, caused by, or of the nature of a physical or mental disease

Pathology : It is the study and diagnosis of disease relating to cause/etiology, pathogenesis, structural alterations of cells and the consequences of changes.

Pharynx : It is a part of the digestive system and also the respiratory system.

Phygocytosis : Involves the ingestion and digestion of microorganisms, insoluble particles, damaged or dead host cells, cell debris and activated clotting factors.

Physiology : It is the scientific study of function in living systems

Plasma membrane : It is the layer of cell consists of phospholipids and proteins acts as barrier against flow of materials inside and outside the cell.

Plasma : The straw-coloured/pale-yellow liquid component of blood with blood cells in whole blood in suspension

Pleura : The serous membrane that covers the lungs and lines the walls of the chest and the diaphragm.

Posterior : Located behind a part or toward the rear of a structure.

Pregnancy : It is the fertilisation and development of one or more embryo or foetus, in a woman's uterus.

Proximal : Nearer to a point of attachment or the midline of the body.

Rees-Ecker regent : It is a diluting fluid used for direct thrombocyte counts; contains sodium citrate, formaldehyde and brilliant cresyl blue.

Reticulocytes : They are immature red blood cells, typically composing about 1% of the red cells in the human body.

Retina : A light-sensitive layer of tissue, lining the inner surface of the eye

Ribonucleic acid (**RNA**): It is a molecule that performs multiple vital roles in the coding, decoding, regulation, and expression of genes.

Septicemia : The presence of pathogenic organisms in the bloodstream, leading to sepsis.

Serum : The clear liquid that can be separated from clotted blood and is without clotting factors, whereas plasma is the straw-coloured/pale-yellow liquid component of blood with blood cells in whole blood in suspension.

Skull : The skull is bony framework of the head.

Sphygmomanometer: is a device used to measure blood pressure.

Spinal cord : A long, thin, tubular bundle of nervous tissue and support cells that extends from the brain.

Stethograph : It is a device used for determining the movements of changes in the air pressure of chest.

Stethoscope : It is an audio medical device used to listen to lung and heart sounds.

Superior : Something which is higher in a position.

Systole : Contraction of heart

Tachycardia : Rapid resting of heart or pulse rate over 100 beats/min.

Thalassemia : It is an inherited blood disorder in which the body makes an abnormal form of haemoglobin.

Thrombocytopenia : Refers to a relative decrease of platelets below the normal range in blood.

Thrombocytosis *:* It is the presence of high platelet counts in the blood.

Thrombosis : The formation of a blood clot inside a blood vessel results in obstructing the flow of blood.

Tidal volume is the volume of air taken in or given out during normal breathing

Trachea : The trachea or wind pipe

Tuberculosis or *tubercle bacillus* (**TB**) is a infectious disease caused by *Mycobacterium tuberculosis* characterised by chronic cough with blood-tinged sputum, fever, night sweats, and weight loss.

Tympanic membrane or ear drum : A cone-shaped membrane that separates the external ear from the middle ear.

Uremia : A clinical syndrome due to renal impairment associated with fluid, electrolyte, and metabolic abnormalities.

Urethra : It is a small canal that extends from the neck of urinary bladder, in male, penis acts as passage for both semen and urine.

Vagina: It is a fibromuscular elastic tubular sex organ and has two main functions; sexual intercourse and childbirth.

BIBLIOGRAPHY

1. Agur, AMR and Dalley, A.F., Grants Atlas of Anatomy, 12th edition 2009, Lippincott Williams & Wilkins, Baltimore. A Wolters Company Publication.

2. De Robertis, E.D.P., De Robertis, J.R., Cell and molecular biology, 18th edition 2011, Page no. 14-16; Wolters Kluwer Health Lippincott Williams and Wilkins publication.

3. Goyal, R. K., and Patel, N. M., Practical Anatomy Physiology and Biochemistry. 15th Edition, 2011. B. S. Shah Prakashan, Ahmedabad

4. Hall, J. E., Guyton and Hall Text book of medical physiology. 12th Twelfth edition 2011. Elsevier publication.

5. Kumar, V., Abbas, A., Fastu, N., Aster, J., Robbins and Cotran Pathological Basis of Diseases, 8th edition 2010. Elsevier Publication.

6. Moore K. L., Dalley, A. F., Agur, A. M.R., Clinically oriented anatomy. 6th edition 2009. Wolters Kluwer Health Lippincott Williams and Wilkins publication.

7. Pal, G.K., Pal, P., Textbook of Practical Physiology. 2nd edition 2005. Orient Longman Pvt. Ltd.

8. Seely, R.R., Stephens, T.D., Tate, P., Essentials of Anatomy and Physiology, 4th edition, 2002. McGraw Hill publication.

9. Tortora, G. J., Derrickson, B., 13th edition 2011. Principles of Anatomy and Physiology. John Wiley and Sons Inc Publications

10. Waugh, A., Grant, A., Ross and Wilson Anatomy and Physiology in Health and illness. 10th 2006. Churchill Livingstone Publication.

www.ingramcontent.com/pod-product-compliance
Lightning Source LLC
Chambersburg PA
CBHW081919170426
43200CB00014B/2767